POEMS 1980-1994

John Kinsella: bibliography

BOOKS

The Frozen Sea (Zeppelin Press, 1983)
The Book of Two Faces (PICA, 1989)
Night Parrots (Fremantle Arts Centre Press, 1989)
Eschatologies (FACP, 1991)
Full Fathom Five (FACP, 1993)
Syzygy (FACP, 1993)
The Silo: A Pastoral Symphony (FACP, 1995; Arc, UK, 1997)
Erratum/Frame(d) (Folio/FACP, 1995)
The Radnoti Poems (Equipage, UK, 1996)
Anathalamion (Poetical Histories, UK, 1996)
The Undertow: New & Selected Poems (Arc, UK, 1996)
Lightning Tree (FACP, 1996)
Graphology (Equipage, UK, 1997)
Genre (prose fiction, FACP, 1997)
Poems 1980–1994 (FACP, 1997; Bloodaxe Books, 1998)
The Hunt and other poems (FACP/Bloodaxe Books, 1998)

AS EDITOR

The Bird Catcher's Song (Salt, 1992)
A Salt Reader (Folio/Salt, 1995)
Poetry (Chicago) – double issue of Australian poetry
    (with Joseph Parisi, USA, 1996)

JOHN KINSELLA

POEMS 1980-1994

BLOODAXE BOOKS

ISBN: 1 85224 453 4

This edition published 1998 by
Bloodaxe Books Ltd,
P.O. Box 1SN,
Newcastle upon Tyne NE99 1SN,

First published in 1997 in Australia
by Fremantle Arts Centre Press.

Bloodaxe Books Ltd acknowledges
the financial assistance of Northern Arts.

Cover printing by J. Thomson Colour Printers Ltd, Glasgow.

Printed in Great Britain by
Cromwell Press Ltd, Trowbridge, Wiltshire.

CONTENTS

ACKNOWLEDGEMENTS

Poems 1980-1994 contains most of the poems I wish to preserve in print from this period. This Bloodaxe edition differs from the Fremantle Arts Centre Press edition of 1997 in two respects. *The Frozen Sea*, originally published in 1983 as a *livre composé*, was my first published monograph; as with my early journal publications, it was published under the pseudonym John Heywood. It is reproduced in full here, including poems reprinted in *Night Parrots*, and in this Bloodaxe edition those slightly revised later versions appear in place of the original 1983 texts and not in the *Night Parrots* section. Two additional poems have also been included at the end of the book, 'Night Seeding & Notions of Property' and 'Skeleton weed/generative grammar', from *Erratum/ Frame(d)* (Folio/FACP, 1995).

My first poem to appear in a literary journal was 'Lucretia', in *Westerly*. *The Book of Two Faces* was published for the 1989 Bookworks Exhibition at the Perth Institute of Contemporary Art (PICA) in 1989 as a result of a collaboration with the artist/sculptor Mona Ryder. 'Zimmermann' was primarily written during 1988 when I unearthed Tewsley's translation of Zimmermann's *Voyage Round The World With Captain Cook* in the collection of rare books at the University of Western Australia. It was intended to appear as a section of a book but never found its place. Revisions and additions were made through to 1994.

Minor changes – primarily grammatical and typographical in nature – have been made to *Night Parrots, Eschatologies, Full Fathom Five* and *Syzygy*. One poem from *Night Parrots* – 'Lasseter on Former Lives' – has been removed. 'Wireless Hill' contains poems mostly written between 1992 and late 1994. It is intended to be read as a separate volume.

Acknowledgements are made to the following magazines for poems included in the 'Uncollected', 'Zimmermann' and 'Wireless Hill' sections: *The Australian, The Bulletin, Calapooya Collage, Mattoid, Meanjin, Midday Horizon* (Round Table Publications), *Northern Perspectives, Nimrod, Otis Rush, Outrider, Printed Matter, ReDoubt, Scripsi, Takahe, Waltzing with Matilda, The West Australian, Westerly* and *The Windsor Review*.

I also wish to acknowledge the Western Australian Department for the Arts and the Literature Fund of the Australia Council for grants and fellowships during which many of these poems were written.

This book is dedicated to all those poets and non-poets who have helped and supported me during the last fifteen or so years. I wish also to express my gratitude to Ray Coffey, Clive Newman and Wendy Jenkins at Fremantle Arts Centre Press.

UNCOLLECTED POEMS

(1980–1993)

Translating

To drown through the moon
Is to feel the white cloud
Swallow a winter tree
On a fresh spring wind.

Cormorants

those perennial apparitions
of the backwaters – their shadows
the faded sails of anchored boats

Slight Air

The others have left.

I squeeze a fallen nectarine
through the wire of a cockatoo's
cage – both prisoners – preserved,
the heavy smell of summer fruit.

Flat by the Sea

I

There are the white walls,
that fresh-laid carpet smell
which could take months to fade,
clean ceilings despite red wine
beginning to spoil, a penultimate
entropy, the window box is bare.

Four layers of six, iron-girded,
cemented into the one solid block,
without perspective. Salt has chafed
the skin of window frames, guardrails,
and door handles ... frosted glass.

Often day edges its way under doors
and breaks into darkness, comforting,
strangely peaceful, it stretches out
from its foothold and settles itself
randomly – a chair, a face, a painting.

It is the place where an old man
wanders the walkways opened to sea,
his face that of Grünewald's Christ,
and in a thick voice chants
along with the dull thud of the waves,
'It is fitting that He increase
and I diminish...' over and over.

II

Ours is the first
in a long line that climbs
up and over the hill

and though others
do their best to crouch
low in its wake,

away from the weather,
driving winds, winter seas,
at least a part of them

is forced to nudge its
gaze over ours by virtue
of the land's incline.

III *Sea Rescue*

Somewhere out there beneath the smoke
a pleasure craft is burning to the waterline.

On the horizon's edge, straight out
from the harbour's mouth, sits a larger
vessel – a container ship.

Overhead, an aircraft lumbers slowly by,
curving back through its flight path.

Flares, mirror signals and facsimile
pleasure craft combing in-fleet. Nightfall.

Onlookers wonder at the thickening smoke,
thicker and blacker than darkness.

In amongst the feeding embers
a knowledge that sooner or later
fire, smoke and hulk will be lost.

Wheatlands

I *An Old Lady Recalls*

We all still feel
the jump of the heart
in catching headlights
rising out of the closed roads.

Or on hearing the fox
bark in the Needlings.
Though I alone recall our sister
hanging the washing with stockings
on her arms, pale skin hidden
from the midday sun.

II *Three-in-One Parable*

The old fox looks into
the sky which is wider here
than anywhere, while the hunters
sing with their fox whistles
the Song of Asking

during the day warm spots
settle in the folds of hills,
at night cold winds funnel
deep into the dreams of sheep.

III *Lightning*

A child poet
my cousin drove madly
through the storm

a fire had broken out and we could just see
the flame on the edge of the world's curve

I was shocked to find that things burnt in the rain.
Maybe it was dry over there?
Rushing home something fell from the back of the truck
and I was pushed out to put things right

lightning struck close by and it shook me.

Sarawak Calendar, 1949

Loading logs at Sirikei on the Rejang,
Logging Loba Kobang, the green furnace,
Swamp forest, the ramin logs ... and they
Smiled at the agricultural education
Officer, and donated to the rural
Improvement school, and pitied the girl
Who'd been a prostitute during the Occupation,
Now shunned by the black-skirted Dyaks.
They felt their munificence, felt their goodness
As it dripped down through the veins
Of rubber trees, stretched out over
The planet as tyres, galoshes, French letters.
He crept the darkest places from the beginning –
Stowing aboard ship, shot in the head and
Reported dead at Gallipoli, unwinding
The spiral of desert, the slough of jungle.
He sold dolls on Sydney wharves and founded
One of those unsung empires – small enough
To be forgotten, large enough to affect
Hundreds. Bloodbrother to a head-hunter,
Receiver of a blade with umpteen switches
Of hair on the hilt – he'd sucked venom
From the snakebite wound, drawn the fire
And poison into himself – he posed for his
Photograph with his arm about the shoulder
Of a tapper, staring deep into the camera.
Mem chastised the maid for entwining her
Flowing hair in the discretion of the tea-towel,
For cleaning the silverware in sand, for
Saying that it got things really clean ...
Young white Mem, proud of her husband
And outback good sense, persevering despite
The isolation ... preparing meals in the homes
Of her servant girls, touching the delicacy
Of the place – straining to hear its muddy
Workings, the rumblings of the long houses.
In the calendars of Sarawak and Borneo, 1949,
She stands on her own, looking down on the
River mist and gold epaulettes of the British

With the sun in her eyes – maybe she is thinking
Of her brother-in-law the philatelist, who is
Forever writing to remind her that for Christmas
He'd like the complete set of the current
Sarawak, Brunei and North Borneo stamps
      In mint condition.

Salmon in a Can

The salmon in a can is as pink
As the wave it set upon, suspended
In a sea of air-conditioning,
Always singing a processed song.
The waters cool, the nights long,
It passes its time floundering
Or swimming against the vacuum.

Dispensation

What does Providence care
that mummified slaters
collect in the corners of its room,
that love lapses on the head
of a match, dead and heartless?

What does Providence care
that a cactus flower
crippled by the first chill
is used by itself to foil
its blackened rot down?

Or that the Marvel of Peru sweetly
occupies and consumes –
squaring the Heavens off with every
flower unleashed, while the limp
sails of a cutter come too close
to the coast – the tide darkly
tugging – dispense a sullen breath?

Birth Notes

Beyond the lace-webbed window
a box tree moves its shadow
stiffly with the breeze.
Flights of Senegal doves indulge
in a kommos of small talk and flight.
I read your innocence, joy
come of the pure tear, the hand
that cannot feed, that cannot summon
even the most vigilant observer,
and regret the seed already
planted within the heart,
the pinpointing of every corruption.
But, for now, the warmth
of your breath smothers all fear,
even the chill in the air
soothing; I offer this kiss
                              as the life
of my own thin blood.

The Day of the Firefeast

Dressed in plastic, the tomatoes
resist frost, ice at their heels
a pedestal reflecting the creeping light
of daybreak. Nearby lettuces burn,
the liquid fire that would halt
the feast. A magpie, friend to none
but its own, prises the flaking sheets.

Spring's harvest. The hindquarters
of a rabbit keep the cat on its feet,
head and torso lolling in its jaws,
its fur immaculately kept, as if
the kill had been doused before
the act, before the sun clotted
fur to skin. The severed rabbit
is also bloodless, its twin halves
as neat as tomatoes in their plastic.

Crane and Hawk

The crane, eyes fixed, moves steadily,
its expression one of quiet desperation;
awkwardly graceful, it lifts
with an arc of its wings.

Turning and cutting the same path over,
the crane relies on what *we* know as *patience*,
while the hawk effortlessly shadows –
death's mimic playing with time.

Between the two, a world rife
with speculation turns uneasily
on its tightening axis; within,
there is something too perfect.

The shudder of the crane stretching,
(the rhetoric of expectation?),
could be an updraft seized mid-flight
and fallen by the way...

What end when a bird of prey
moves so slowly? When a crane would seek
no more than a circuitous life anyway,
and the day warms to indifference.

Magpie Larks

Magpie larks are almost skittish:
unsettled, withdrawing into themselves,
you could diagnose split personalities.

Tilting, swallowing their voice,
you'd expect them to turn full circle,
flip the world back on its shoulders
and lift it pertly up again.

Mildly aggressive, they suggest threat,
and are often seen on the tails of larger birds,
though make light of a pursuit
which may finish as abruptly as it began,
almost convincing us ornithologists
that such acts are games, that life is really
as light-hearted as we'd like to think ...

Though sewn into the black and white
of their patches is the solitary codex,
their gatherings small scale,
and even these tentative.

An Irruption of Ibises

You spoke of more than five
and less than ten ibises taking
to the space between shed and orchard,
that they skimmed the frayed tops
of citrus trees and alighted
with a clatter of beaks.

Daily I pass and search
these grounds, my theory of irruption
seeking to unravel the irony
of forbidden fruit, of the land
of plenty, of the blind leading
the blind, of tainted oranges,
the mist of an uncertain migration.

Dispersal

To be sitting and looking
up at the scarp
                with trees bolt-upright,
almost like fright, and catch
a windhover on the periphery
of sight, barely definable
in its suddenness, and lose it
amongst the sheets and foliage
of a rank old paperbark,
pigeons dispersing like a gale
from their roosting place.
The shock – as the pinpoint
accuracy of lightning
strikes at nothing:
                this hunter attracted
to a collective body warmth,
settling snugly –
ignoring its prey.

On the Half-life of Cuttings Fallen Short of Water

The stems seek the water
of the vase, only to hover
above this sustenance,
attempting to draw an extra life,
augur beyond the pruner's knife.

But starved flowers decay
and deprived buds fail to bloom;
as their brittle calyces atrophy
foliage sheds in the sunless room.

Ambivalence

Ambivalence
                            moves with you
as you pass
                     flowers of cowslip
hanging
                  like limp champagne flutes
pulling their yellowness
                             slowly
from splinters
                 of sunlight,
as you pass
                the corpse of a dog
on the edge of a puddle
                          the muddy water
lapping
            at its dank coat.
Ambivalence
                  is the plantain
                             opening
cracks
            in the timbers of a bridge,

and a river
                    heavy with rain
                                        cutting
back into its flow,
                         and jacarandas
with seed pods
                         crisped in a cold oven
sighing
                    with the burden of scab
                    (scrofulous lichen)
skeletal leaves
                         showering you
                                             with spores
of mildew.
                    In the shopping centre
                                             car park
islands
                    set in asphalt
                                   -treeless-
                                        spill
lime-scorched earth,
                              and the son
of a teacher
                    who taught you as a child
embraces
                    his load
                              of shopping trolleys
with a clatter,
                    and ambivalence
                                        shelters
in the small spaces
                         where clover commits
fratricide
                    to gain ground,
                                   where
the sulphur-crested
                         cockatoo
                                   perches
behind
                    the optometrist's window,
                                             peering
through rainbow-coloured
                              glasses.

No Through Road

The bush at the end of the road
is earmarked for development – you
don't have to look at a zoning map
to ascertain this. Blockaded by houses,
tracks crisscrossing it are widening.
At its centre are a thin geranium
and a struggling Madame Pierre S. du Pont
rose. Dumped cacti have re-rooted
themselves and are multiplying.
Horses are worked through it daily,
jumping rails cut from jarrah
and lashed over the sandy paths.
Children have introduced corrugated
iron, erected and excavated cubbies.
This was to be the *ne plus ultra* of the suburbs,
the bush at the base of the scarp.
But the no through road is poised
for movement and dynamite has been
heard in the heart of the hills.

Sunspots and Strawberries

the child massacres strawberries
on the carpet
the afternoon making its presence felt
in releasing the sun
to the window
curtain-filtered
luminous on remnant of strawberry,
the child turning its attention to sunspots
attempting to grasp them
always empty-handed

Death Side By Side, from the Top Down

Do you see that tree on the far side
of the creek? he asked, pointing with his
cabbage-stalk walking-stick. *And my neighbour's*
mandarin trees? And those in my orchard?
And do you know why? why the leaves yellow
and die from the top of the trees down?
First the side nearest us, then the other?
I kicked at the ground and guessed dieback.
Pah! he said, *Dieback, what is this word?*
What matters is that trees are dying
because humans do not understand. This
is of our making, and it is we who die
from the top down, one side and then the next.
We have sucked this poison from the soil,
have nurtured its growth with greed
and ignorance, and now it is larger than
all of us and won't take 'no' for an answer.

Everlastings

A couple pick flowers
while their child lies
cribbed in the dry rustle
of stalks & petals.

Everlastings persist,
though some limp
with storm damage,
or even broken-necked.

White   pink   rose   scarlet
cool   almost ice   their swayings
but the slim tip.

Bees, laden, pay no attention
to the pickers, slow-moving
vessels half-submerged
in the rippling waters.

The breeze stirs the feeling
deep inside the painting,
the sun flickers
& is passed over
by pumice clouds, bunches
hanging rigid in the shade,
mock-glorious in their brilliance.

Interregnum

1 *The Sound of Oranges Falling*

In the ripening the falling is laid,
the sound an impetuousness, impact
the heavy-lipped loaming soil wanting
firm skins to yield. I am told
that during an *interregnum* high winds
will sever fruit at a distance, and I
have seen it fall, though never to lie
and await the measured call, bell stroke
made as regular as breath, the tree's
weakening grip. The sound of oranges
falling counts sleep out of absence,
almost obsessive, too close to count
as breath, distance accepting death.

2 *The Fly Impales Itself*

The larva of the case moth
drags its construction
across the footpath

reaching the edge
it overextends
and teeters, its head

and front legs
wavering feverishly
I move it to safer
ground.

The cicada transfixed
on the tip of a palm spear
moves its wings and legs
slowly

I prise it free
and am not surprised
to see it make ready
for flight.

3 *Clouds Comb The Hills*

Come close again, read and reread,
the fine print clarifies when the clouds
hang low and comb the hills. Liquid
prongs scarify, reach out and scour
the breath. Vision is clear – the sun
removed, myosis does not contend with its
overload. I walk the lowlands and count
the sweeps, marsh ground that sinks
another inch every year. Who belongs here?
A black cockatoo swings off the tip
of a widow maker, shrills out from the fringe,
a rival for the bush telegraph. The cityscape,
a waterhole that refuses to fill, despite
the clouds combing the hills, our prayers.

4 *Catharsis: Crows Over Winthrop Hall Tower*

Pyramid on a plinth, crow-tipped pedestal,
a black halo that settles and lifts,
settles and lifts. Sun, on side, cuts

a curvilinear flight, marks a timetable
with beat and off-beat, the slow lungs
and retraction of wave-motion wings.

Interregnum: distance measured, come
apart, we settle and lift, settle and lift.
Black halo that would drive us apart,
should be the garland, the unravelling
of tower and flight, sun and sight,
over the tower of Winthrop Hall, ignore
our flight, our tight-lipped concentration.

The Roundhouse Manifesto

In this most
uncompromising
of stone buildings
love can and will
effervesce
over
the bludgeoned rim,
the pocked limestone,
and spill into sea.
Suffering
is a minimalist trick
shot through the minds
of beachcombers
sweeping
and re-sweeping
the narrow shores,
shot through the minds
of voyeurs eyeing
a plunging neckline,
the gentle breakers.
Suffering
gives ground.

Is there beauty
in the sheer?
Does the lyric
retain
intensity
when sounded
from bone pits
and quarries
of the soul?

Salt
keeps
the ledgers,
takes inventories
of prisoners
warders
visitors
stones
slotting
into place
shackles sitting
neatly
on their chains
set firmly
though
not perfectly
into the walls.

Salt's graffiti
entertains
the governor
on his
short visits,
teases
the harbourmaster,
watches over
their interests,
allows no room
for escape.

The Roundhouse / Cornucopia Nexus

Sanitised history neat in its decagonal barrel,
neat with its whale-death tunnel: cornucopia,
the plundered horn breathing the cold stone
of its seafaring goodwill, this harvest of plenty,
this foaming over at the end of the world –
the convicts, Nyoongars in transit, prostitutes
& drunks, the citizens, & the place staying
intact only because the harbourmaster
thought it a valuable windbreak for his house;
cornucopia, like love, like sunflowers
rooted in stone rising up over the walls,
kissing the salted air, sea's camaraderie;
cornucopia – when the town takes history to the
cleaners, & feels it has a licence to print money.

Windbreak

You wouldn't believe wind skirmishes
in this narrow corridor – you'd think
it would shoot straight on through
without giving second thought to contesting
the size and shape of its boundaries.
But here is the evidence to the contrary –
bean plants and capsicum bushes flayed back,
the undersides of leaves exposed to the sun,
their edges charred like burnt manuscripts.
And to make matters confusing, the chaotic
rearrangement of life implies that some
sort of crossfire has taken place – the wind
fighting against itself. So, now shadecloth
doubled over has been used to line the corridor,
to tip the odds in favour of the civilian
population, to pacify the wind in its confusion.

Black Suns

The orchard, canker-bound and fading – Australian
Gothic. A bladeless windmill remonstrates

with a warm wind as it singes
oranges scattered in bitter wreaths

of deadwood, scale, and vitrified leaves.
A black-winged kite wrestles with temptation

and logic, water rats scaling the ruins
of barbed wire fences. The season equivocates.

I remove my shoes, the water stretches
bulrushes like new strings on an old guitar.

I position the wreck of my body and wait.
There is arrogance in this – expecting

him to appear, to consider his withering fruit,
divine my return, while refusing to cross

and help drag black suns from their sick zodiacs
with the hook of his walking-stick.

Brambles (in memoriam)

I journey through drafts
of an old poem
& find an image
that draws us
together
in absence –
brambles, stray
on the banks
of the Blackwood,
yielding sweet fruit
though rolling
in bitter-sweet coils
choking the forest,
closing life out,
unravelling like watchsprings
sprung from their casings
& left to corrode
& collect
on the workshop floor.
But you, who cleared
your property
with the slasher
to prevent
the council
dousing
it with poison, are
no longer here,
while we,
fruit gatherers & lovers
of thorn & confusion
reminisce over blackberrying
& life in the shack
at a time
when absence
was simply distance.

Epistle to Veronica Brady

The moment's world, it was; and I was part,
Fleshless and ageless, changeless and made free.
'Fool, would you leave this country?' cried my heart,
But I was taken by the suck of sea.
KENNETH SLESSOR

Tranquillity cuts its teeth
on the sails of yachts spread
thinly on the river, the bridge
sheds its scales, King's Park
sparks out, the Monument
returning the narrow path.
The frailty of the water,
ribbon winding inland,
crustaceous path, though little
moves amongst the banks.
Though don't worry,
the true face floats
below the surface,
the watertable
with a case of acne.
When love draws freely
cross-season, without boundaries,
you must expect the residue
of pleasure cruises
frescoing their movements
across the shore. Near
the University, powerboats
skip a beat and laugh,
yachts ride high
upon their paths,
wakes move slowly –
but it is the sea
and not the river
that pollutes the heart.
And the Furies are
but effervescent shrimp
that burn their way unhindered
despite the nets.

Rowers

Gunwales shudder as looms
strain against thole pins.
Despite it being summer, the morning
is crisp and the body brittle.
The shell splits water and casts
it under, the coxswain eyes
a southern pillar of The Narrows Bridge,
sets the rudder, and calls *stroke*.
A yacht gybes against the rowers'
defiant course – unwavering,
linear, sharp. The sailor,
looking back over his shoulder,
divines luck in the lifting blades,
his reflection cut and dispersed.

Escape

it being easier
to escape
from the infirmary
he removed the spring wire
from the trigger
of a window-spray atomiser
compressed
and bound it in layer
on layer of cigarette paper.
after swallowing
a good half-hour passed
before the paper dissolved
and the spring burst
into his stomach lining –
darkness escaping,
light denied entry.

cameos of love and access

1

denied access to language
love erupted like a radiator

battling against a forty-degree day
& a dodgy thermostat

2

only the hedonistic
can illuminate an act of love:

conspiring superior locations
& valuing extrication

as much as landing a clean
& home-hitting orgasm,

but pleasure, responsible
for its own PR,

rates sleaze as kink
& exotica as sophistication!

3

the cottesloe beach mobile
shifts gently under the light

fitting – it's cold outside
but the red plywood sun

lifts their game
& works better

than tanning lotion.

4

jealousy is like spanish fly,
spiking the body –

an irritant
that's raging

out of control, a fetish
that defines its ground

but relishes leaving it.

5

dispossession is when a wild hand
intercepts your low-to-the-ground

hyped-up and fizzing proposition
and sends it whining

straight at you: there is
a kind of

gratuitous pleasure in this.

6

their marriage was a set
of five-year plans: a drop

in consumables but product
outstripping prediction

in the military arena.

7

purple swamp hens leave
the tyre-wasted wetlands

and come uphill towards
power-lifted lawns: they

see it as a good omen

and spend the day
in the garden.

8

guttural – of the throat:
in fine voice are sung the praises

of exclamation & gratitude.

9

lemon picking from branches
overhanging the hardiflex fence

the weird guy next door
glances sharp & deep

into the eye-like window
finding the soul

less naked than
he'd like.

Keeping the Garden
Alive / A Sense of Place

Summer's coming on so I drive
back home every couple of days
to douse the garden – the house
musty and the water in the taps
stale and tasting rusty. Sometimes
I reconnect the phone and call you –
yeah, the garden's fine though
the grass has grown long
and the landlord forgot
to give a key to the plumber –
a calling card says he
couldn't get in.
You know, it's like
visiting a museum or catching
up with a past life
on a scratched and yellowing
super-eight movie. Even
the light up here seems different.
The bottlebrush flowers
are losing their boldness –
lashes of thin blood
dulling in crazy piles
over the skeletons of snapdragons.
In the shed, a furnace
in the midday heat, my paintings
are flaking. What do you
expect? I can't face moving
them inside to a cooler
place. And I can't
bring myself to touch
much in the house. Yeah, a museum
or filmset or scene of a crime,
where every item must remain
in place, as evidence
of a previous life.

Long-necked Tortoises

Despite
looking like the hulks
of destroyed tanks

they are the victims
of war, their shells
the homes and civic
buildings
of a routed
town, a slow
siege from an
enemy
engendering
a false sense
of security
and then striking
arbitrarily

Upturned
and gyroscopic
on the verges
or as flat
as chessboards,
parquet
for traffic
to slide over
homeward

Crossing
from one pond
to another,
their long necks
bobbing like camels',
they reach a gallop –
and intensify
their danger:

working against
that slow myth
they excite
the latent predator,
the driver with a lust
for the peculiar,
like the hunter
searching out
the last Tasmanian Tiger,
the unique trophy.

Adieu

The lack of technique scares me.
The similarities and differences
scare me.
                I have flown across four states
because I've been scared, have known
my limitations, and know that poetry
can only be drained from a fragile
body when the mind, a poor adhesive
anyway, releases your meagre
frame to the wiles of the taxi driver,
the whims of the dealer, the cunning
of your voice as it mimics
the lyric of a drunk
pretending to be dead
in a fine hotel bed
at the break of dawn.
                        Yes, workshop
this: an incest victim eager
to tell his story in the Kiwi Bar,
a Swiss traveller bragging
about the quality of his country's
pharmaceutical companies,
a bunch of lads down from Byron Bay

whooping it up – the Bay a bore now
it's fallen victim to the target audience
of a Saatchi and Saatchi or John Singleton
advertising agency – I can't remember
but believe me, they told me
and told me with conviction.
No, you can't make poetry
out of anything – unless
you bind glittering images with lies,
or let false sentiment buoy sweet words
out of dark moods.
                    Remember, the smoked glass
of the bar is smoked only through absorption.
You pour and it drinks. There's
no technique in this. But you can't blame it.
This place is in recession. Make the best
of your opportunities. Adieu.

Notes from Southern Seas:
An Allusion to Love

Rock dome, spiritual centre
or outpost where observatory
limestone coaxes the electric
sea, fork lightning driving
a printing machine
with cadmium rollers,
[this the rub, an experiment]
mixing the urgent turquoise
and feisty emerald inks
of liquefied antarctic
wastes, the white-wasted sharp-tops
and de-capped breakers,
spray-flash and freak-wave-levellers
congregating about the spits and juts and cleats
of old granite and gneiss.

And O, the chemi-luminescent wonder
of tiny man-o'-war jellyfish,
mainsails fallen membraneous heaps,
miniature gondolas with inflated,
bladdered hulls, all indigo and purple
tints: azurine tendrils
arcing like gelatinous
wire, larger than any beach
or ocean, even Southern
and prone to exaggeration
by its own confession,
or the mezzotint
of memory, this metonymy
this distant welding of land, sea, space, minutiae,
and discretion.

THE FROZEN SEA

(1983)

The Frozen Sea

To see a World in a grain of Sand
And a Heaven in a Wild Flower:
Hold Infinity in the palm of your hand
And Eternity in an hour.

WILLIAM BLAKE,
Auguries of Innocence

1 *The Frozen Sea*

having cut a hole whose size
is as big as we can make it, we peel
away the light and submerge ourselves.
that darkness lay below the ice
(excepting the shadow of light)
seemed strange: I had always thought ice
to be clear, nothing more than a misted
transparency; and though assured
from memory that there was none
other than drowning to fear,
I could not shake the thought
that some hidden end was near,
an end not connected with water.

2 *Links*

Every separation is a link...
SIMONE WEIL

I

There are days when the world
buckles under the sun, trees blacken
to thin wisps, spinifex fires,
and white cockatoos, strangled
in telegraph wire, hang
dry and upside down.

II

I think only of thirst.
The drifting sand does not
lend itself to description,
the sketchy border trees
offer little protection
from the sun as we negotiate
the edge and fine line
between sand and vegetation.

III

I have always lived by the sea,
or travelling underground, have always
been concerned with water – the flooding
of mines, rain in dark forests,
the level of the tide.

IV

To see a waterbird, maybe a crane,
fly deep into desert, comes as no
surprise – we note its arrival and follow
its disappearance, discuss it over a beer,
and think nothing more of it.

V

And nights, contracting into cool winds,
when the sand becomes an astrolabe to the stars,
where in the reflection of the crystal spheres
we wander without direction, searching out
water flowers ...

3 *Aviation*

I **South**

an airship wanders past my window
and out to sea, an ocean-going liner
of the air. curving south it could be
seen at point d'entrecasteaux,

or later, amongst ice-packs in antarctica –
with memories of southern cliffs
mere rocky traces, black patches
sown with pivoting seagulls.

II Mid-point

helicopters hang over their pad,
we circle the aerodrome and fall
away, our direction undecided,
confused by the ever-present hum
of heavy engines, the sucking
and blowing of air, the pattern
of faces pressed against windows.

III North

you rise up to where the air is clean,
not the dry air of desert, not the heavy
air of mangroves. a spotter plane hangs
low in the sky, heavy clouds appear on weather's
eye, the wings bump, the coast passes by.
watched from a landrover, a glider catches
an updraft, the sun like ice, a drunken
lazy flight in fine weather.

4 *Early Recollections of the South-West*

I

Point Peron
became my gateway
to the South

there, channels
opened themselves
and crabs were found
in dozens under rocks

the reefs littered
with opportunity

helmet shells
gripped to this wonder
with every ounce
of strength.

II

Busselton jetty
stretched to
infinity –
            surely
icepacks guarded
its end?

we clutched our fishing rods
and thought of sharks

a mile out the gaps
between the planks
grew larger

III

at Prevelly Park
we rediscovered the reef
and conical shells

there, an emu
emptied the bin
and my mother read Milton
for an exam

i grew giddy
and cut my leg

IV

of Augusta
there remain
slippery rocks,
waterwheels and periwinkles,

from there on
mum and dad
were always apart.

V

the stink of dead whales
reminded me of my grandfather's
smelling salts

Albany, in all its beauty,
held a great emptiness,

the treachery and darkness
of its cliffs and dark sea

made me think of shipwrecks.

VI

Pemberton,
a timber mill

seeping wood
and the smell
of burning

as planks and waste
plummeted from the chute
a workman winked at me
and i felt strange

VII

there is an
imaginary line
that forbids fresh fruit
travelling any further

'fruit fly'

and then towns
pass by almost
instantly – a Neptune sign,
four square store, and children
who have spent a lifetime there.

5 *Surreal*

going back through the months
along roads i recross rivers
and see alive what i then saw
in death

we hurl along karri-headed laneways
playing scarlatti, vivaldi –
                                        strange
intrusions, the sun banking through shadows,
the silver top of the forest shimmering head-dresses
a hundred feet up.

6 *Lucretia*
(for Vanessa)

still shackled to our moorings
dragging ankles in a brown river

there is a
recurring vision
of permanence

though we still catch
the ripples of passing
boats

7 *anatomy of a fall: a parody*

the anatomy
of a dead seagull
falling past my window
with its back to the sea
revealed itself in striking
cement three storeys below.

the climate within my window
was forming hurricanes, humidity,
like a magnifying glass, distorting
my view, though clearly I could discern
its inelegance – splayed and buckled,
a heap of bloodied feathers, certainly
the result of an imperfect dive.

8 *fragments from A World Without Water*

the water has changed,
its new appearance a well-kept
secret

reduced to skeletons
things underwent the myth
of equality, naked
before their neighbours

    *

in dust, lands have joined
and new borders must be
drawn up

with space up for grabs
a new colonisation
swamps the imagination

war threatens
to fill the waste

    *

in prohibition territory
they're running bourbon
that looks and smells
like blood-in-water

by the quart it's a thousand
but there are them that's
willing to pay

and considering the risks
(AGENTS FROM THE KALAHARI/SAHARA
VEILED AND FEARSOME)

the bootleggers
defend their price

      *

thirsting, does she want him for his blood?
for his body juices and receding veins?
this lady thinks like a vampire
(her blood is dust but his might be water)

she smiles a cracked face, stretched lips,
wry smile, holds her hand to a solitary
white breast (she's been saving it)
         and drinks deep...

in his every step searching for the well,
his divining stick erect and waiting,
she senses the loss of moisture,
the drying of their love.

      *

he welcomed desiccation,

we are the dust of the universe
he told them.
         they stoned him.

he went to his lover
and she comforted him –

in the palm of her hand
he was dust.

9 *Orpheus & Faust – 2 Legends*

I **Orpheus**

his head appeared in the hand
of a beach-comber...

amongst the netting,
a gathering undetected

by the inspector
of illegal catchings,

they found the head of Orpheus
snow-white and out of place

amongst the stains
of a bark-dyed river,

brown and heavy with mullet.
they pondered its fate:

release it to drift
down to sea,

or dry in the smoking room
with the rest of the catch?

II **Faust**

illuminated by lighthouse-thrown beams,
slices of a night sun, i wander from its strength
to a ragged and indecisive finish, linger
at a rainbow's extremity...

this is where i wander,
i searched and longed for it,
followed its fine thread out
through darkness, tracing
faces in the silver nightcaps
of the sea ...

and here, slipping
to an uncertain end,
i stay, wavering amongst
the frayed ends of your
russet hair ...

10 *The Image of the Wickerman*

in the wickerman's head
there is another

through his eyes
burn eyes in shadows

his blank gaze and supercilious grin
hide an appreciation of colour –
        We label him the Object.
his legs, arms, torso, and head,
are packed tight with objects –
a choir singing a strangely
hypnotic tune,

the voice of the sirens
rises from our scarecrow.

11 *mimic: a blindman's view of the sunset*

an orange sunset
sets the skin tingling,
the effect and feeling
is orange.

numb with cold
it slides a strange
pair of blue hands
over the flesh.

adjust the speed of the skin,
set the aperture of feeling,
draw sun sky and all into
that black old camera −

see through the back of your eye.

12 *the conjurer: it's hidden in his pocket*

he's hidden the sun in his pocket
and tied it in tight − at night
he plays out the day under
coconut-shies, gambling
on his quickness in
deceiving the eye.

13 *Love in Isolation*

consummation
was out of the question −
his *ideal* balanced delicately
between Leda and speculation
of what might have been
in a perfect world.
to grasp her flesh
and call it his own
would have meant an end
to everything.

14 *Desert Fruit*

the desert in spring
edges its way
thru two worlds

the fading fruits of spinifex
and wildflower

the night parrots glide
thru a night-lilting sky
and break away to the east
having crushed this fruit
over their hard tongue

guided by memory
and the smell of water
they settle on the banks
of shrinking rivers

15 *back thru the looking glass*

smoking swans thru our white hookah
i too have felt Alice playing
on the edge of sanity,
her nimble limbs
feeling their way
thru woodland streams,
cooling themselves
in spring waters ...

16 *The Return*

the ribbonweed tugs at the river mouth

the wind against me, i must tack away
and direct my course towards
a reconciliation ...

17 *The Quay*

inner city dreaming
feeling only myself
walking in stiff clothes
and feeling the cold

the taxi whirling
past terrace houses
down through the city
curving buildings of glass
into the harbour

I stare warily
through a flaw
in the window

dumped on a grey morning
I find myself watching
a small boy hauling
ships into the bay.

18 *Distance*

only I remember
the soft distance
under the hills

the shadows of birds
and trees falling away
into fields,
          spreading
like spilt red wine
after an easy summer.

19 *Epilogues*

I Epilogue in a Canyon

broken underfoot, sheer faces
and ragged parapets

few explore the rise
and fall of this

shot–hole canyon.
they say it breaks away

from its mouth by the sea
and heads inland

into secret deserts
where only smell

can find its source,
the liquid of its mystery.

you piece steps into spaces
and destroy your curiosity

back at camp the others
pray for a clear night

surely morning will reveal
nothing more than a dead end.

II Still Life / Thru a Window

through a window
away from the sun

the sky glows
in heavy passover

stretched out
the ribs of its frame

an oval, green lake
of cricket pitches,

players floating
in slow movement
to the wicket

a man building his tomb

through the stiff windless trees
his head is that of a cricket ball.

III **Saints in the Terrace**

hear their breath
a light breeze curling
through the cloister
their hair standing
with a shiver

bound in silence
the cold sits on them
like a robe

a wolf howls

they cover their arms
and stop breathing

20 *an unexplored lake...*

trees cling so close to its shores
that we are forced to imagine its beauty...

ZIMMERMANN

(1988–1992)

Heinrich Zimmermann was a 'common sailor' on the
Discovery during Captain James Cook's final voyage. In a
little-known account published in Germany in 1781,
Zimmermann records his views of both this voyage and Cook
himself. Zimmermann had succeeded in smuggling his notes
past the English authorities upon arrival back in England,
only to have his *Voyage Round the World with Captain Cook*
relegated to obscurity. Zimmermann's observations of Cook,
and especially of the events surrounding his death at
'O-waihi' in 1779, reveal an honesty that is lacking in the
more 'refined' versions that are available.

Zimmermann, Anaxagoras,
& The Great White Whale

They first caught sight of it
in a stream of cold between
Van Diemen's Land & New Zealand.
Zimmermann had been working
on deck when the sky lit up
brilliantly. Some of the crew
were blinded & wandered overboard.
A vision of Anaxagoras appeared
on the horizon & the ship
leaned towards its impenetrable whiteness.
But the Captain, his wits intact, hauled
in the sail & pushed hard against
the compass. The last they saw
of the beast was its white-metal body
dipping into the line of evening,
a great white whale
submerging.

modus operandi

storm

he said to himself – *all is calm,*
only the body balks at the gale,
only the body stretches & grinds,
blue devils in the bulkheads,
the timbers squalling. but the mind
is calm, the mind is the eye
of the storm, the mind is an anchor
that dragged through unfathomable waters
will hit no reef nor break free.
all storms pass – & even wreckage
makes flotsam & jetsam – nothing
is lost in destruction.

becalmed

Hope, shredded like sails
flown in high winds, lies strewn
around the decks.

Lethargy eats like dry rot,
the decking powders underfoot.
The wheelhouse is unattended,
the tiller flounders.

Becalmed, all manner of cruelties
are imagined. It helps
pass the time.

entertainment

some of the crew think punishment
is the only entertainment
they're likely to get at sea.
Maybe the Captain knows
as much about this
as he does the body's
need for vitamin c.

isolation / navigation / bad jokes

an astrolabe stretches the distance
between clusters of stars to the point
of capsizing, the ocean's raw

& enigmatic breath moves the sails
like smoke-damaged lungs, the cabins
rife with tobacco & semen.

Glass

Glass – brilliantly coloured,
fused to granite – caught his attention

on an island supposedly
uninhabited, unvisited.

He tried to collect a sample
to take back to ship,

though found it would not break,
& when touched became as stone:

blank, colourless, inhospitable.
As the sun had almost set

he prepared to return, though turning
away heard the glass singing

& was frozen where he stood,
his heart filling with night.

Grace

The indications grew steadily worse.
There could be no doubt – a leak on both ships.
The heat on, & the Captain indifferent.

The atoll frothed – more & more
of the crew reported sick.

Samples from the jungle's fringe
proved disturbing, though Banks
marvelled at the growth rate of palms.

In three days they watched a world change.
Even the sky fell heavily red.

Zimmermann gripped by electric fleas.

But then Grace dropped by silently,
filling them with iodine.

Clear of the place, Cook warned them to forget
what they'd seen – the tropics will often
addle the *delicate* European.

a dead sea

the sea swelled, though rising
only in the vicinity of the ships,
like an equatorial bulge,
the wooden hulks still births
in a bed of blood & protein.
Cook looked to Zimmermann –
a *common man* – for explanation.

Zimmermann Organises a Dance for the Women Villagers and Syphilitic Sailors

They chose a spot near the beach –
open, though fringed coyly with palms,
the white sand like the burning snow
of Home. And bonfires were kindled early
despite the heat. The Captain, as usual,
turned a blind eye to his crew's frivolity.
It was agreed those most severely
diseased should have last choice,
with the exception of the officers
who, of course, would go first.
The Chief & his warriors had seen
the ship's cannon in action
& were impressed. The Captain
had also handed out trinkets.

The dance was a great success
& the warriors kept away as promised.
Zimmermann later had to confess
to getting a little tipsy & missing
the *grand finale,* when couples
plunged into the surf & cleansed
themselves. None got back to the ship
on time, leaving the Captain to spend
a lonely night, for which he let his
displeasure be known, forbidding
such reveries for a fortnight.

The Sybarites

The sybarites maintained
that luxury was only
in the eye
of the
beholder:

they coddled & pampered
Zimmermann – blowing perfume
over his hammock, whispering
sweet nothings

He asked if they were
his forever –
                      No,
they replied
as the ship
began to roll
& pitch,

*We work our way
into all myths,
at times when hard-going
makes even dreams
seem a luxury*

*The truth is we take
the minor players
& split them like grapes
between our teeth.*

Cook's Anthropology

Ball-bearings in the brain cavity:
some spilt from Zimmermann's ear hole
& were swept under the carpet by
an astute Captain Cook. He ordered
the pouring to continue. The other
specimen (collected from an island
North of New Zealand) was only
semi-reamed – though, for the records,
cleared of all substance – & filled
halfway to the top, or halfway
from the bottom, though who's counting?

Zimmermann on the Politics of Cook's Death

O-runa-no te tuti
Heri te moi a pop Here mai

Disease-thick, these islands
drink adamantine fires
the hot god under the mountain,
the fear written into the face
of every sailor, the payback
blood, & that's hot too,
though if Zimmermann
thought the god Cook
cruel & ruthless
he also held him
a model to all.

The natives
move like smoke,
trashing trinkets,
making iron daggers
from anchors. They
dance in his clothes
& ditch his hat
off the mountain,
returning only part of him,
having eaten the rest.
The god Cook is not dead,
but sleeps in the bush,
& in the morning
he will return.
He wouldn't hear
of Providence
so nor does the crew.
The officers seem glad
to be rid of him.

Zimmermann & The Press

Rushing to file their stories
before an Apocalypse severs the lines:
Yes, Zimmermann remembers the late Captain well;
Yes, Cook was fond of clear days, though not
    unreasonably so;
Yes, Cook's relatives ARE threatening to sue:
Yes, Zimmermann claims that Captain Cook's spirit
  is: i   fertiliser
     ii in danger of being mined
     iii undergoing electrolysis
     iv cryogenically preserved for future research
         with an eye to possible revival
     v often heard crying.

THE BOOK OF TWO FACES

(1989)

The Book of Two Faces

They paint themselves every morning
before going out
            though people remark
on their clear, natural complexions.
            This body art is no mere distraction
                        no theatrical prop
                        no prompt from the sidelines
of a hidden life, the wings of a chintzy circus
                        no façade to impress, disgust,
                                    incite fear
            and definitely not art for art's sake.

  Love? They would deny it.
  Rationale? This they would also deny.
Occasionally, they frequent galleries – or hesitate
when passing a street artist doing ten-dollar head shots.
And the covers of popular magazines make them blink twice.
  Though not Janus.
Never Janus.
  The chips fall, the gamers clear the tables.
The cards lay themselves out in their particular
patterns. Two faces, their glances never cross,
though each knows the other's watching.
  There is no superstition, no luck.

Something out of a book that has yet to be
made into a movie – the printed word so flexible –
            on the big screen, the television.
Though it's inevitable, considering the evidence
            of duplicity.
                        The nose quivers
over the neat lines of cocaine. The pages
of the book rolled into straws – the two faces

            twitch and look almost ugly.
Some call them beautiful without having seen them.
            These are known as the book lives.

74

Late nights are not tax write-offs
        though fingering their tumblers
        of whiskey you'd think so.
                        Why else bother?
nouveau nouveau nouveau you say
                        take my word for it,
they'll consider it a compliment, and anything else
for that matter – at one time or another
they've all been styles.

premonition
is not
unheard
of in such
circles
in fact
just to mix
with them
requires
a certain
amount
of this

no explanation
can be given

enough
has been said
already

Page 333 of *The Book of Two Faces*
lists them boldly in black letters.
It says they've been coming out of their shells
(despite the social life
they're a nervous couple – business and pleasure
should not be confused) lately.
                        Up until a few years ago
their number was silent.

Luck would have them draw their opposite

from the pack (of dreams), though in drawing
themselves fate is contradicted. They
cannot be seen together – the rules are stringent.

It is up to us to keep an eye out,
                              look for clues...

At the theatre
they can hardly fail
to be noticed – lying on a table backstage
                    or poking their noses over jacket pockets
                    or nestling in shoulder-bags.
As you can imagine,
                      there are times when they almost
come face to face,
                    though, like fingerprints, no two sets
of faces are the same.

The Two Faces Sketch Book

a relic
religious dossier
codex
instructions to the apparatus
of false eyelashes
masks pivoting on the stem
of a goblet

          when the sun
at its highest point
(observed from the heart
of the quadrant)
          illuminates
the dihedral head
the cloud sheets of make-up
false eyelashes
twin faces

    The two faces
have replaced the city's mask –

the climate of a growth
fuelled by the guilds
and hierophants
of the four estates – the constabulary
                    the media
                    the retailers
                    the labourers

    The two faces
wear contact lenses – iced, mirrored,
        filigreed with gold leaf

the mathematics of divinity

in a world like Borges's
'Tlön, Uqbar, Orbus Tertius'
where the touched becomes desire
where touch is desire
the compass cuts
an expression
exploits
the plasticity of... object
                    desire
                    expression

Reading themselves   co-joining
with the chair (which is not a throne)

the two faces
covet darkness
the silhouettes
of identical
lives

Has the hit and miss of a joke
fallen
          on deaf ears?

the suites blossom
and adopt forms hideous
to their creators

images
locked in combat
on the fine line
of both worlds

awakening

they taste
the bitterness
of interference

the liquid colder than it looks

Charon moving away from his parents

Charon colder now than the dark waters

the two faces drinking the river dry
and boarding the boat

in search of an elixir
in search of the philosopher's stone

On the Ganges Delta
workers have placed masks
on the backs of their heads
to confuse the Bengali tigers
who never attack
                    face to face

Isis the magician
rides the boat
of reflection
over the sea of the four suites

the vessel could be
the body of Nut
her mother

the night sky

the sea

the points
of tension

the tomb of the two faces
is theatre

on stage they are alive and well
and singing

            maybe at the point
of a coming together

                    maybe on the lip
of an offering to the dead
                the ferryman
                the votive cup

A Requiem for Two Faces

The two faces danced on the lip of the cup
like nicks of sunlight, undressing. And will
you believe me when I tell you that even then
they remained hidden to each other? Though
conversation did take place and they knew
where not to step. Fear mongers would predict
catastrophe. That something so perfect
could not in truth exist. I would like to prove
them wrong, but just as I take this inventory
of dance steps I am sprung – they have in stepping
out again collided and come

                         face to face
                         exposed

                                  confusion
                            setting
                                      in
                                           their
                               faces

      peeling,
            unravelling,
         shot spiralling from their centre/
                                  creating
their own order ... does this make you happy – Logic restored?

Logic taking over? The book writing itself back into shape
       The lines spreading over the pages.
       Make-up and masks made ready for launches.
       Loves requites itself admirably –

                        the two faces
                        labelled –

                              Janus.

NIGHT PARROTS

(1989)

THE FROZEN SEA

Prometheus

Takkana, bringer of fire, little understanding,
little understood, has set fire to the children
of Leda and the Wickerman. Touchpaper, kerosene
to scrubland, has rendered the land empty, charcoaled,
fruitless. And now he explores the fire-breaks
for stray weeds surviving the Blast. Like kilns,
mudbrick houses remind inhabitants of holocaust,
the ceilings dripping asphalt. The fields opened,
their wooden hearts extruded and scuttled. Shelter
from the blaze was elusive – bridges burnt,
rivers dried, wet blankets smoked and exploded
as they tried to cover their tracks. This whirlpool
of desolation embalmed imagination, numbed sense.
The land and inhabitants grew delirious with pain.

Exhumations

We buried them thirty years back
at the town's edge, helix of desert,
when burials were commonplace.

Now, beside this defunct church,
necrosis has crept into headstones:
silent, blank-faced, wrapped

in a rust-light of iron flowers.
When mine-shafts collapsed
the narrowest of paths

could take days to open.
Rescues were nothing short
of exhumations, rescuers – thieves.

There being no careful removal
and registration of each stone, ours
was a sloppy job, by any standard.

Passing the Ruins

The bus driver had said
that the old telegraph station
now covered in drifting sand
was operated by telegraph men
from the two different states
and that they sat on opposite
sides of a partition passing
messages blindly through holes.

Fragment

only the day before we had been
walking along Cold Harbour Road
in weather of the red hawk
and thought of our deaths rising
on the darkened tips of its wings

and as we sat in the shadows
of tamarisk, a willy-willy
kicking at the foot of the dam,
a heron lurched out of muddy
water on unsteady legs
and launched itself
slowly into the breeze
its wings scuffing our words.

Finches

Salt Paddocks

Down below the dam
there is nothing but salt,
a slow encroachment.

Fighting back, my cousins
have surrounded it
with a ring of trees.

At its centre
lives a colony of finches,
buried in tamarisks.

Finch Colony

The leaves, like wire, are so tangled
we dare not venture too far into their heart
where flashes of song and dull colour
betray a whole family of finches.

We hold our breath
and become statues.

Is this fear of disturbing their peace
or of a delicate raid from unknown spaces?

Finch Flight

To join the finch
in his tenuous kingdom
amongst tamarisks,
the hot snow of salt

You must gather
trajectory and direction,
sharp summer flights

Exile yourself
from the wind's hand.

Finch Death

The dead finch lies on salt,
tight-winged and stretched.

The others shimmer
loosely in heat

the salt's white mystery
coveting tin cans, skull of sheep.

Slowly, death rides this hot glacier
further and further away.

Night Parrots

If at all, then fringe dwellers
        of the centre.
Ghosts of samphire, navigators
of the star-clustered tussocks.
Of salty marsh, limestone niches,
        and acrid airs.

If at all, then flitting obscurely
the rims of water tanks, the outlands
of spotlights and filaments of powerlines ...
in brief nocturnal flight, with *long
drawn out mournful whistle.*

If at all, then moths in a paper lantern.

Notes on Fire-tumbles

    I

Fire-tumbles roll inward
from a desert's edge.

At first they appear as
cart-wheeling spinifex,

later, flame beyond sight
takes hold, enthralled.

II

It has been said
their substance is
of lost forest –

breath of dried air
unable to take hold.

Consumed, moved in wind.
Sand.

III

Back through shadow
they stretch sunset
to unimaginable limits:

enveloped sky,
cinnabar of abyss.

IV

Eyes harden and fall.
Fire-tumbles, seen in
vision, last an instant.

In desert the light
of fission lingers.

V

Fire tumbles are not poetry,
nor even a substitute for poetry.

They are things wild
whose wanderings
are without motive.

LASSETER

Prologue: Cloud, Tree, Desert

I

The cloud of Nebuchadnezzar
mushroomed and evaporated.

The veil of pumice and ash,
the incinerated expression.

Lasseter, then of city, had
looked with the crowd into the
sky's abrasion, disappearing sun,
blast echoed in glass.

It was said, even then, that
Nebuchadnezzar had filled the
widening stomach with sackfuls
of grass.

II

The forest petrified, gold
flourished, a new age spoken.

Nebuchadnezzar, coiled tightly,
shrouded his golden image – the
tree on gold grew, watered in
heaven, its speech the rumination
of desert.

III

That early on Lasseter
had turned to yellow lion
to spread word of his
condition.

That later an angel
clasped shut lion's jaw
and bled him white.

That in magnification
of time, Nebuchadnezzar
through yellow lion, learnt
'transgression of desolation'.

With news of Lasseter's arrival,
Nebuchadnezzar, unseen, revealed
sun at Lasseter's feet.

Fire-eaters at Lasseter's Reef

A troupe of fire-eaters
stumbled on Lasseter's Reef

For seven days and nights
they entertained

throwing vast jets of flame
out over desert

Having seen
their repertoire

he grew bored and desired
conversation

but their every breath
produced nothing but gold.

Lasseter Prophesies Camels

Blue, blue, the camels will come,
tink tink tinkling with tiny clocks

encased in sandalwood, tink tink tinkling,
in time, the dust of clocks of sandalwood.

They'd water Lasseter, he guessed,
wouldn't let the xenophobic desert

differentiate between the locations
of its chosen species...

chosen or transpired. The bending leg
hobbles straight, the hump deepens,

thickens and stocks, despite sand,
despite the weight of tiny clocks –

the heavy tink tink tinkling of the
dust of clocks encased in sandalwood.

Lasseter, concluding all of the one source –
he, the water, desert, dust, camels, and clocks,

rejected their offer, and called water
no longer water, but gold transubstantiated.

Of himself and camels – all clocks he thought –
whose tink tink tinkling faded with evening,
the blue camels feeding...

Lasseter and the Red Nebuchadnezzar

He had guessed at seeing
it on two or three previous
occasions, appearing amongst
the brush and spinifex –
a fire-tumble.

Of course, there had been
numerous scrub fires over
the passing summers

but rarely at night

and rarely seen from the rise
of reef rolling deep into desert,
vanishing and reappearing
with sand dunes, burning
without fuel.

Starry Night

And the Nebuchadnezzar
above the starry night,
and still reduced to foraging
amongst burnt seeds and spinifex,
stared far unto night.
His blindness, amused-burning
as he went, meant nothing.
Lasseter's pain was, his pain,
after a time, was nothing.

Lasseter and Nebuchadnezzar's Readings of Faust

And as Nebuchadnezzar plucked the guitar,
misterioso, the night parrots, attracted by
this something out of the ordinary, ringed
themselves on a shadow's horizon.

Still in possession of body
Lasseter turned to the small
indiscretions of soul: the collection
of fuel at the desert's edge,
the abandonment of man.

'Where do you go upon leaving me?'
Lasseter had asked, by now accustomed
to Nebuchadnezzar's nightly winding
of the fire's web.

Lasseter and Nebuchadnezzar's Answer to the Signature of God

Written time over: OMO DEI,
read in rock-carvings, translated
out of Dreamtime. Upon the wedding
of souls and ensuing starvation,
Nebuchadnezzar, who'd held
the world in his stomach, realised
his own leprosy, castrated himself,
remade the animals he'd eaten, and
looked to the chlorophyll of his
hanging garden for votive offering.

Lasseter then set the entourage
of Nebuchadnezzar, brought in
to look over the interests of reef,
in the direction of water and gave
them their leave.

Nebuchadnezzar, having found
he could no longer extend height
further than his wasted body –
the signature of God so altered,
his features barely humanoid –
returned to the grazing land
beneath spinifex fields.

Lasseter Laments His Fall to
the Wits of the Ignorant

He had tried to ignore
the obviousness of his fate – misunderstood
by the ignorant, judged by the ignorant,
who in their need to shoulder or create
guilt would look for circumstance
best suited to this end.

                    And yet
his sight had grown clearer.
And his faith in the Nebuchadnezzar
(who only knew in the brilliance
of his extinguished soul's fire),
grew in their praise of the reef's empty sun.
Were they too 'victims of circumstance'?
Nebuchadnezzar grew unsure.

                    Lasseter grew unsure.
His morality was born of thirst, theirs
of greed. He'd learnt to despise
the sanctimonious, those who felt secure
in reconciling this tainted view
with visions of soul's future gold.

Lasseter the Hypocrite Brings Yellow Lion
Glowing in Mockery at His Desert Blindness

Lasseter the hypocrite. Accuser –
false friend to the Nebuchadnezzar.
He who said, 'You follow an evil light.'

He could find his way about well enough.
He had been blind before and managed, well enough.

O, yellow lion, your brightness
undetected in his blindness, as he climbs for stars,
                plucking greedily, popping
                them into his steaming mouth.

Or, maybe. Maybe he could turn
it back against the antagonists. Consider, if
by accident, he blindly dropped his cigarette
and set fire to the all-too-dense vegetation.

Fable

And Nebuchadnezzar scrubbed
Lasseter's head the whiteness
of snow, scrubbed and scrubbed
until all trace of arrogance
shone less than the dullest
of stars, shone less than
spinifex of a salty desert mire.

O Lasseter, inheritor
of the shrinking gnamma holes,
what time have retreating waters
for such as you? What images
persist beyond dislocation?

Lasseter Predicts Bye Bye

Hadn't really searched out the whole area,
though could guess at the rest. Lasseter
the anchorite. Lasseter in this desert
of untranslatable horrors.

Lasseter and that Dutch woman.

And the Nebuchadnezzar
with his court of fools.

Having a real good time.
Together.

That's it, in a nutshell.

Bye. Bye.

Nebuchadnezzar and Falls

Lasseter: No stream of tears
          stands in this step. Sand,
          burning sand, is the only welcome
          these feet endure.

Nebuchadnezzar: by now ferried into Limbo,
          leads, deceptively, from shade
          to shadow. The spinifex: red foam.

'Onto the burning plain...'
                    Nebuchadnezzar, circle below
                              circle,
                    with Falls, he plunged.
                    Though, in truth, existed no
                              edge.

His form become the water
        become the steam
and all that endure.

The Note Lasseter Would Have Left If Only
the Sun Had Remained in Place

Where to turn upon an evening in the absence of sunset,
when the appearance of a different light makes the place
no longer cynical but empty. The tinge of day
lives in the false light of the desert god,
whose favours are few. Sparingly it lights
its narrow path, woven, all the same, conspicuously.

On the outcrop he picked at the Reef's wounds
with the little hard digging rock left.
Nails, long since frayed.
Long since, O Lasseter.
Long since the Nebuchadnezzar.
Long since the resolutions uncertainty left.
Those long nights since looking to the sun
as guide to a ridiculous glint of idea
            ridiculous glint of hope.
Amuse yourself, Lasseter, with a self-pity
that stinks of the god whose selfishness
leaves others all-too-greedy for the specks
it misses; rare though they be.

Lasseter's Loss Recalled

And if it be time
Nebuchadnezzar, in the fringe of trees,
repeated shadow and moon, came down
on an evening to present illusion
in the carved light, Lasseter
had to accept. The steam, sweat
from the lake's dry basin, lasted
not to overwhelm. And it was heard:
    heal not our burns
    heal not the cause of fire.

Lasseter's Calenture

And waiting to translate
into words, words more sublime
than the last traces of Nebuchadnezzar,
hanging as always on to those vestiges
of shattered, uncollected thought,
he decided not on Name but the
dominance of light-in-thought. How
from these 'slices of a night sun',
he could touch upon a point
that would give validity to fear
of a desert's final, absolute
evaporation. Or, in the extreme,
breaking of mines,
flooding of catacombs.

Catacombs and Fiery Furnace

Below, guessed at but not known
by Lasseter, Nebuchadnezzar picked
amongst the catacombs of collapse,
testing the infra-structure, and on finding
it short of crumbling, issuing forth
embers of his cinerate fire, fiery
furnace: unaccounted-for fires
Lasseter was sure to take as a sign
of return, or in the least, memory
enough to drive uncertainty
into future decisions. Scratching,
admittedly in imitation, the outline
of three men he'd once fed to fire,
born in the self's golden image,
he mused that Lasseter too
would be content in knowing
the Angel of God had plundered
before even a hair had been singed.

De-cap / Volcanic

Lasseter sewed the lazy lip
of volcano smoothly together
satisfied that through mimicry
of restraint the reddening clouds
would be humbled. Long time they'd
fed on its scant eruptions – accumulating,
refusing to release even the slightest
recognition of consumption. Lasseter
awaited the Solar Belch. Regardless,
the clouds brooded, and furthermore,
the volcano gained a new restlessness:

the sand gathered heat and fused
with a sea of glass, Lasseter absorbing
the glut of his own reflection. He chipped
at the volcanic lip, but still the Whole
maintained. What now Lasseter?
Which way to turn? The clouds hungrily
waiting – dry and heavy – the desert
heating to the point of cracking ...

Lasseter's Recollection of Lost Records

And thus he came,
and thus he answered
rude questions with alacrity,
as if for no other reason
than to pass an evening
out of place with suspicion.

And he'd taken it from days
when he and Nebuchadnezzar, beneath
dark moon of rocky overhang,
conspired words whose order
would prevent compromise
in calling this or that vanity.

And they'd burnt with Nebuchadnezzar.
And only Lasseter lamented, and did so
without suspicion – a loss, by his own
definition, not hard to cope with.

Lion, Rainbow, Cave

I

Lasseter and lion, in light
of cave, rainbow –
                recess of hand
                recess of head.

The pockets of pyrite,
half-light of blasted ceiling,
fissure spread threefold – of Lasseter,
Nebuchadnezzar, lion pining.

II

Startled, birds scatter
on a border of smoke. Everywhere
the red eyes of the winged gargoyle,
the predator, reflection of an old
Nebuchadnezzar.

Paroxysms of herb given
by lion to Lasseter in his
grief for Nebuchadnezzar, reduced
rainbow to strips – peeled, secured
in dust of cave, unvisited lake,
scattered mulga, quartz outcrops,
sandhills, mallee, saltbush plain,
limestone, ironstone, gravel, the
scattered ash of blanket.

Lasseter Ends in Fire

After Nebuchadnezzar, and the sympathy,
he had felt a renunciation of greed. He allowed
the light of reef to fade.
                        But the fire,
in its evening race along the scarp
rekindled a reliance, a pity greater
than his own, a notion of suffering
as nothing more than pride. A fool's pride,
the fool's whimper for the consuming fire,
and a golden thought that seemed to help
bring about the necessary catastrophe.
By association, the regime of Nebuchadnezzar,
of fire. Unstrung comes the epic,
                        by association.

Lasseter and the Holy Fire

Nebuchadnezzar, beyond
Lasseter's dream, detected
a woman, body washed transparent,
eyes of pale geranium lake. The dream
of reason produces monsters.

Ergot swelled the seed
of desert. Movement in-sphere,
parhelion, mock sun in halo, lifted
not just a little light
from surrounding ground.

Burning hands, dilated feet:
the persistent itch of gold,
miasma of body. Agents of greed
conspired fall of reef.

In shadow, so called 'airy thinness',
transmogrification by Holy Fire
into something fed on darkness.
His steam risen, effluvium to
opportunity hunters – those Usurpers,
Users, and Imitators, who'd searched
vainly for remnants of empire.

Pugilists Put on a Show

By now, all had crumbled –
stratas shed and even
the mirrored reef
no more than shard.

And on hearing of Lasseter's
disintegration, the pugilists
came to put on a show
with beer and parchment gloves.

The night parrots arrived
(the last recorded gathering)
and chit-chat struck between
the blows. The dull thuds,

the pivoting and shattering
embrace – all wheeled and turned
as the sun deflected
their hollow blows.

THE SHAPE OF THINGS TO COME

The Shape of Things to Come

I write: the vermilion paint
on my hand is scarlet under today's sun.
The breeze pleasant. The vegetables, healthy.
In the writing of 'I' the projected lines
become senseless, formless. What follows?
A dirty vermilion. Shutter-clouded room.
The sun, passed over. Yet, there is judgement.
And idea derived. In the wreck of vision,
in the wreck of a desire to project
a knowledge of changing colour, sun, garden.
Like gargoyles, above the eaves, crouching
over shapeless rot of garden. Sun: vermilion.

Rivers of the Homeless

The Builders sought space
and removed the foreshore,
one must sleep closer to
the hazy, oily water now.

The electric storm designates
disorder as the cypher – brilliant
calligraphy that bristles from
red turrets, the distant bank
of shattered glass. A gloomy
by-product exudes from the shadows
and you loosen your sweaty clothes.

And eventually, lulled by the wasting
rainless storm that seeks moisture
in the skin, flesh, and bones, you
accept the fate of the Exposed. Asleep,
asleep the fallen thunder, churning
propeller of a boat retreating inward
from the sea, mouth of river.
The boatswain calls and calls,
his voice rasping through sleep.

And the twenty-year song churns
in the eye of storm, and sharks approach
up-river, threatening the pitiless
ankles of the Stygian angler.

Moon, Trees and Desert Wind

Forget the impropriety of trees,
of their fixed leanings and predictable shadows.
The moon, strange places, and a cold desert wind
present a visage that too easily can be taken
from place and carried amongst the worthless
symbols that adorn your kit – the few obsessions
that have come to comfort a knowledge of survival.
Accept that a sack of rice offers far more
than these bending trees: elusive memories
which, at a distance, multiply in scorn
and lose whatever value, whatever sustenance
for depleted, emptied souls they'd had.
Empty are the forerunners to collapse.

Chess Piece Cornered

Mice in the eaves, and breathe well my dear.
Breathe well my dear, mice in eaves in madhouse.
Breathe well in this   space
                                      solitude,
                                                      breath never
sweet breath, that lends me not
to the small persistent clutter of mice,
river long, and this, your breath
hard to find. Mice in their short breath
heard only at night. By the vent. By the pillow.

Sick Woman

Don't. Crow and butcher bird
    over garden
    over sand
    over me and sick woman.
Don't.
        Of sick woman, butcher bird
brings crow to ground, crow or
butcher bird fall, brought to ground
by sick woman. What is it we feel?
A draught, maybe as we catch
the falling crow or butcher bird
by sash of light, sash of window.
Sick woman, and me told I look
like a little yellow Valium pill,
rising to the scuffling crow,
butcher bird, sick woman.

KITES AT SELCUCK

The Black Sun

As the morning rises out of the city's
Trailing archipelago and over the first trains
Breaking ice on their cold steel tracks,
We shall walk down past the blackbird trees,
The shadows of buildings close pressed,
The dull eyes of the Unknowing.
And as you head North, I'll leave
The station, follow your rumour
Through the dark clockwork of winter,
Damp market place, squalid streets,
Acacias by the harbour. And like
An ambassador called home at time of war,
Step onto an Eastern ferry, always knowing
That a black sun hung over our parting.

Samos

I

It is funny how at the time
you can never get close

you skirt its shores, discover
rocky grottoes, climb terraces
of citrus trees, and watch packet ships
sail through the gentle cliffs
into the main street harbour.

II

Or in the evening, drinking the island's
wine in a small waterfront tavern, watching
the last workman pack tools and head home
up into the old town from the site
of a new tourist hotel.

III

And as you travel through the olives
over the island to the town named after
Pythagoras, you wonder what sounds
will herald the approach of Turkish sails
out of Asia, under the perfect smiles
of a ruined fortress's wind-swept poppies.

On Caryatids

Whose function can
only be ornamental
according to those
met with steady face,
solemn intent, who've said
that quite frankly they have
enough trouble supporting
their own weight.

Kites at Selcuck

Standing on the side of a crumbling road
wondering where I would spend the night
after a mad day battling television Turks
selling magazines, hasheesh, and bits
of ancient Ephesus, an old American post
office van pulled over and offered me
a lift into Selcuck. Pressed tight against
a man with a gangrenous hand, I was laughed
over, hugged, and invited into half-a-dozen
homes. Dropped at the bus station, I found
none of the hagglers I'd been fighting
for days, but a moment of prayer, dusty
minarets, and a group of bus drivers flying
            home-made kites.

In the City of Kaks

you walk down the street to be
shot up by a pharmacist

your room is littered with food,
broken ampules, books, cigarette butts,
foils of mandrax, dexedrine, spots of hash

your chest is so tight that you can
barely speak or move

you lie on your bed, always waiting

it is overcast, and as you
glance into the street below
the last glow of a diseased sun
catches eye and window

and you think of Ted Berrigan
who said that he died of Pepsi and pills,
and of Robert Adamson, who was quite taken
with the idea that Berrigan had died

                              of Pepsi and pills.

the kaks, on the windowsill, always laughing
at these, your small crimes.

Luna Silens

Fazar and Zohar

Have not gone to bed. Still awake
on dexedrine, staring at my Euripidean
Electra: red paint/ indian ink.

Zohar registered in a dream.
Awoke, had breakfast. Museum –
sketches of demon gorz, morning star.
Six pieces of toast, pot of tea.

Line of sugar ants starting, or ending,
on the cupboard top, where sit remnants
of watermelon.

Asham

I watch my friend move across
his bed towards his 'Bengali boy',
the shadow of roof fan chopping
their faces, parting their bodies.
Neither is 'master of the situation'.
Theirs is to leave things up to
the breeze blowing in through
the fly-screens, to follow its
wavering intensity, the
sounds of Dhaka it carries –
slow sordid movement of rickshaws
as they pedal through the cries
of Asham, horns, and kaks.

Maghrul and Esha

Dusk. We sit in our room. The red
Dhaka sun sits at the bottom of New
Elephant Road. A fight breaks out
in the hotel foyer. I read lines
of the poet, Syed Ali Ashan –
   'I smelt all these corpses
   And I articulated their voices
   The voices of their living days.'

Tonight will be luna silens.
After curfew there shall be nothing.
The final cries of Maghrul
have reached us from the minarets
of Old Dhaka; we, stationary,
await the only thing remaining
to a night emptied of life: Esha.

Charybdis and the Rickshaw-man
in the Sea of Dhaka

He does not understand Charybdis.
Though can we be sure of this? Could it not
be said that he deals with it well? Considering.
Though his heart must skip the occasional beat.
And has anyone seen him without that frown of sweat?
Sweat? Cycling charybdal pedlar. Pedlar of Charybdis.
Funnily enough, through allegory it could be explained:
the blooded eyes of the charybdal sun, the sun-embattled
sea of Dhaka. Charybdal military. Students
and politicians of Charybdis. Wit? Unquestionably.
Of the dryish sort. Amused by the clean. Rickshaw-man,
peddle us nothing but contempt.

Varanasi

The Balcony

In the city of ghats and great pilgrimages
I sit on my corner balcony listening to the chants
of the fruit vendor as he pushes his cart
through crooked streets, watching pigeons
fly down from a large pepper-tree
into the open window ledge that sits
at the foot of my bed.

A Note

Recovering from an overdose and dysentery,
I flick through the pages of various
books bought a few days back, annoyed
that I had gained so much pleasure in
unwrapping their hard covers. Two nights
ago, during delirium, I could not get
Raskolnikov out of my head, an image
far more vivid than that I have of
the small boy, hopelessly mutilated,
dragging himself down to the Ganges.

Blériot's Flight Over the English Channel

Calcutta – during a respite – I read
of Blériot's flight over the
English Channel. I'm not sure
if there is much in this – I could
draw comparison, or make moral
allusion, to the 'Telegraph – Mode
Survey' on whether or not 'Calcutta
Is Dying', or to its beggars who
only live on 'by the grace of God'.
But I think not. Instead, I should
laugh at our absurdity – two youths
nibbling at chunks of tepid melon,
trying to maintain their strength,
not vomit over the room's tiled
floor, which the manager says
looks like the marble
of the Taj Mahal
if polished.

CINNAMON QUILLS

Warning to Mandrake Eaters

The mandrake enjoys
the womb-of-the-earth,
that pushes tightly
its stagnant birth.
Fragile in their Marat's
skin, the constant
bath of soil that keeps
them stretching.

Tapping dark strata,
enclosed, risen over,
the shape denotes
the human feature –
not the mandrake
that screams for life,
the scream is from
the eater.

Blue Roses

> *On the Government granting funds*
> *to create blue roses with a long vase life.*

The prototype
    blue rose
lasted longer cut
    than any vase.

Grecian urns had
   turned to dust,
holocaust greened
   the earthly mass,

though, a blue rose
   there was,
a demigod to the froth
   and gas.

Of Wooden Finches

Painted thinly red
the wooden finches said –
'Sing us, and we shall sing you,
the room dazzles and almost shimmers too,
let your hallucinations shed
a finch or two.'

A wooden bird flies
from me to you,
flies in and through
the darkened room
and swallows me
and swallows you.
It flies into
the darkened room
and alights its
wooden tomb.

And it almost rained indoors
as she fed the wooden birds
what he could not restrain –
her tears, her kisses – he
could not distinguish – so he
turned to song, and the wooden
finches sang, sang their
wooden song.

The Irony Almost Stings the Sense

The taller crow caws,
riddles the smaller's brain;
when the older crow caws
the younger caws the same.

Though the caws are different,
and no two caws the same –
the irony almost stings the sense
enough to caw again.

Cinnamon Quills

The wreck foundered
on the foam ropes
of coral troughs
and jungles

and sailors rose up
gripping the buoyant
clouds, screaming –
'Foulplay! Foulplay!'

The cargo shed itself
tumble by tumble
into the sea.

Cinnamon quills
(according to the
inventory) tossed
bobbing together
mistaken for a raft.

THE DANCE MOVEMENT OF BEES

In the Best Interest of Strawberries

Not at all predictable, strawberries.
Begun earlier, this would have been
    nothing out of the ordinary,
    nothing more than a justification
for the slow creep of a not so long ago
    dormant strawberry. Though now,
after abstinence, brought about
in uncertainty and delay, they have
begun their creep, in bursts. Transplanted,
they shall reach the edge of grass, the
threat of tangling, eventual choking.
We can only survey their movements, attempt
    to curb frustration with our coaxings.
If we do not witness, a hope should be
    held in their eventual fruiting.

Fall of Windchime

A pair of robin red-breasts,
solitary blue wren, touch
of shattered windchime.

In so immediate-a-space
the barrels – six planets, confidence
shaken, fell to a mediocre wind.

And the rainbow fell
upon the triptych of trees,
panelled: clouds supporting
angels supporting clouds.

Scattered. Mummified rat,
late fallen walnut. Apropos.

The scurried particles of water.

Frost. Cold fingers apropos
hands. Windchime fallen,
cold cut of water.

The Cut of Broccoli

I

On land recently thirsty
for the decadence of rain,
land not yet satisfied
with the ignominy of extinction

the luxury of a toadstool's appearance
loses distinction. Pale blue caps
whose warmth is for the cupped hands
of children and the inquisitive.

II

Of my thistle shrine
a new harvest has come
upon whose spikes
the fallen are replaced.

Someone has called this
the 'tyranny of years'.

III

And it is cut   she
in–stigmata,   blood of broccoli,
cut in the turning flame

of candle.
            The slugs
have gathered in the garden.

IV

The descent of many small mustard-coloured birds
in quick angular flight, upon the decaying grape,
the wreckage of a late neglected harvest,
was sudden. An instant saw both exploration
and plunder satisfied. I too removed myself,
clutching the excited bundle of a cat
tightly to my chest.

Of Frost and Sun

If we step quickly over this hill,
at the point of red gum's opaque spillage,
we shall enjoy two sunsets –
this, and that of a lesser hill,
shallow hill whose hewn walls,
dome of mirrors, to encourage winter's
light, capture sight in cuneiform.

And having mentioned this love
she pointed to the eye
resting unsteadily on the line,
the reddening within the bottle.

An evening walk into the smoke of town,
quarter moon, the burnt hills gathering

frost. Of the sun – a red straining –
they prepared to walk its contrary path.

He had addressed his fears time over.
He had looked to suffer and expected

his fear to be played against him. Confronted
with fear, it seemed that no dignity
could come of downfall.

The frost bit hard at their wandering sleep.
Not the first to have fallen, they declined
the travelled path. The chill of waking,
frost and sun punctually replaced.

Prelude to Dissertation on a Flea
(not a Wyeth)

The would-be rotation
of the passionfruit flower
that could have become the
nagging headache, that
could turn carousel,
spilling ants, tossing
counter-weight, hair
almost the colour of dust
or retreating sap, rusted.

The wind flattens the barbed seed.
Moss powders, hovers, instantly
disperses, tanks spiral towards
the expected aridity – just
the moment, the point finite,
awaited, hungered. The siphon
turns its rasping coil, sucking,
sucking… a dry recess beneath
winter's glassy pool.

'Is it drawing?' 'Why no water
when I hear it gurgling, sucking?'
Water dries and hardens a solid
emptiness in these parts ... the frost
mocks the would-be dust.

And at the lip of an old well,
the rim of tank, bank of stream
and river, edge of soak, brim
of pit, old fungus gathers
in on itself, the dried coil,
the withered crest.

Dissertation on a Flea

> *For he strove in battles dire,*
> *In unseen conflictions, with shapes*
> *Bred from his forsaken wilderness,*
> *Of beast, bird, fish, serpent, & element,*
> *Combustion, blast, vapour, and cloud.*
>> WILLIAM BLAKE,
>> The Book of Urizen

I *fumus terrae*

Without name, sung are movements
of smoke strung out over glass,
watery grave of flood-gum. Oil
of insecticide. River, reflection
deceptively clear, river, coded
mirror, tinderbox of valley.

O flea, entombed – the yellowing
foam of wrecks and bones, the
cryogenical poison – on bank,
weather warm, earth-smoke rising.

The bamboo kite positions itself
beneath its tether, suspended
threadless, imminent.

Of tulip translucent to vein,
in hothouse, of the twice seen
yellow barn that became the yellow
wheat. *Pulex irritans*, human flea,
product of bloodless pit, festers
at their swollen feet.

II   *out of ovarium*

Eve's organs nurtured the germ
of humanity. Moon, broken cycle,
division an uncertainty. Calibration –
to no avail.

The belly adopts the attitude
that it can only become so large.

Of serpent, fish, bird, beast, recorded
beast, fish, bird, serpent. All cloud,
visage pale, the poet incarcerates
orange trees. Defined as lymphatic.

Of original sin the flea judges
from the swirling tree, the breaking
ulcer, eggs cracked between fingers.

III   *cloven blackbutt*

Rain holds back, cloud occluded,
the beast would seem to inhabit
clear sky, the world rebuilt in
opposing action – Cain and Abel,
detractors of grain, preservers
of flesh. Fireflies transfixed to
entomologist's window, pinpricks
of sky. Cluster upon cluster.

The dog with yellows, a different
glow again, struggles through
mouthfuls of toadflax. This the
worm sown down, serpent hidden
from child. The clouded boundary
of self, the charred orange
of blackbutt.

IV   *the lightning tree*

The endive – late flowering
centre of azurite – brought them
from all corners of the garden.

On days struck in the flint
of storm there arises a need
to associate the illogical rub
of cloud, as atmosphere within
atmosphere begins its shift.
To relocate anew. That in lightning
reddened figures dance the dissolution.

Mark expression not of face
but hand, the rainbow snake's
perfect existence. For the cold-blooded,
the warmest place shall spiral anew,
anew the reflex of unfelt sense –
spasm coiling, binding point of tree.

V   *O siphonaptera*

Carrier of forbidden fruit,
make not your hidden purpose clear.
O siphonaptera, feed no solution
to these, your curious victims.

VI   *nine birds descend*

Do not speak of birds
presiding over Orc's birth,

of the yellow-winged honey-eater,
the impossibility of an opposite.

That prevented the hand becoming
part of a greater tension.
Of red-eyed blackbird, iconoclast.
Of silver-eye or finch-a-dance
on funeral bath. Fantail, spread
in sun, not the scalloped hand.

Of butcher bird, crow, and fallen planet.
Of Daedalus and Icarus swollen in sea.

The fluidity of half-lights stopped
them in their tracks, repeated in
an instant, the wedged flock flew
in ash, the feather of molten ash.

VII   *façade of water*

These, the decorations of a well watered
place. The bird plunges, star-eyed, carnage
of oasis. Mosquito poles its raft
with unravelling leg.

The first strokes accepted as formative.

Caught, an ant stumbles the rotation
of passion flower, apex spinning hair
the ambiguous colour of failing sap.
The barbed seed fled, fleas turn in
dust to breed, the world erupts.

In spiralling mud an artesian frog
defies and takes breath, aged breath,
breath of fetid air, slow miasma –
its soundings, the music of pit.

Water 'enriched' in poison of field,
blank tableau, medium for production
bypassing growth. Sun, stripped of
colour, defies focus – the dead
described as no more than dead:
florescent wheat, undetectable in
bendings of heat.

VIII *in sensorium*

In sensorium fleabane
brightened the turning wheel,
pinhead wagons, trails of vanishing
thread. In sensorium evening
separated the paper wing, torn
flesh of once-used sting, evidence
of a bee's suffering. Flea, in
sympathy replied, 'Time's Infernal
Concert' – stars plummet, restrainer
ropes stretch and sing, the
ringmaster drives his circus
on to greater things.

IX *ghost of a flea*

Flea, fed on tempera, ghosted
down its body. Crushed, following
a similarly erratic path. The
opened mouth buckles, hooked tongue
hardens and extrudes – whisk, whisk,
ghost spills ghost in cup of blood.

Left to multiply in the corner
of a room, flea-spirit comes
of human waste, and waste
breeds waste again.

> *And their thirty cities divided*
> *Inform of a human heart.*
> *No more could they rise at will*
> *In the infinite void but, bound down*
> *To earth by their narrowing perceptions ...*
> WILLIAM BLAKE,
> The Book of Urizen

Come Black Frost to Cineraria

Pale faced, she sits stitching loops
into the belly of Ecce Ancilla Domini.
He, back to the window, light ending
in lattice-work of hoped-for
impenetrability, faintly visible.

Of corridor, tepid air, stagnation
of cineraria. (They'd measured in step
the distance, always disagreeing.)
He mutters a sympathy, she acknowledges.
Beyond, city devours city.

Despite retreat from lowland, frost
had tracked its way through cracks
under doors, between floor boards,
flaws in the ceiling. Come
the failure of scented geranium,
the snapping of artichoke column,
osmosis of daffodil, its presence
was felt in vast silences, dilation
of cineraria.
                    The trees emptied of life,
a temporal fruiting, he tracked inner
movement with guesswork, approximation.
Wound down to end, each leaf the dented
planet.
            Black frost, no further than screen
of hyacinth, trident of moon cactus.

The Dance Movement of Bees

I

To the bee
the red light
of the city
is colourless –
window cleaners
slide up and down
the blank faces
of skyscrapers
and peer steadily
into the sun's reflection –
dancing the dance of life
for the pencil chewers
watchers of the incandescent
for those who whittle time
down to the quicks
of their fingers

as the day warms and unsettles
clouds redefine the dance
from honeycomb to hidden sun

II

The chrome-green
thin trunked trees
in prisonbar rows
so close that even
surface roots
intertwine   drip nectar
wantonly
              the clouds remain
                    fixed lifeless
          between hills and thin beaches

III

A bee trapped in a train carriage
staccato on the flat glass windows
until let loose over the river
the carriages rocking
                    rattling
                    shaking
                    trembling
over the trestle bridge

at stations bees hover
reconnoitring front yards
of daisies and ground-cover thymes,
looping the loop   or almost
the hooped stamens of wattle cones

Surfboards, prams, miniature headphones,
earplugs tuned to the races
the barbed wire
running at eye level,
          obscuring
the rare white hibiscus
which to the bee is a fountain
of colour   a map of nectar

and the train passes all places
suited to the bee –
factories for roof racks and differentials,
fencing products and tyres,
steel pipe and transmissions,
and on the new estates
the poplars and pencil pines
sidestepping fences

A swarm settles in the rusted pipes
of spent wash-houses
in trees split with past storms
the eaves of new and old houses
the folds of scrap metal yards
or in Moreton Bay figs
that have spread
over entire gardens

IV

On the city's edge
amongst semi-rural backlots
bees descend
having danced
amongst the hills

seeking the river mist,
cooling their hives,
directing flights
between chuckles
of unseen kookaburras
drawn caws of crows
hanging in solitary
couples

V

The skies clear,
the sun left cloud-stained
bruised violet

bees cluster
in the half light
unable to decipher
a river broken by ferries,
the tightening railway tracks,
the blurring of bridges
and skyscrapers,
the diminished scents
of shrinking flowers

gravitating slowly
towards entries
dispersing the brooded airs

NEBUCHADNEZZAR

(for Arthur Boyd)

Trope

The wind blew and picked
at the dusty cavities
of reef ...
        Elected, reprobated,
Nebuchadnezzar's prescience
had been of Lasseter,
and now, left to himself,
even guilt and resentment
lost meaning ...
           left to himself
he cast meaning to the clichés
of desert –
       to the hessian walls
and watertanks strapped to the
bulging flanks of camels,
to the dryblower, pannikin,
pipeline of sand,
to the swampers and barrowmen,
to Father Long and his camels
and the lump of emptiness
made sacrosanct in its
'Imagine what this could do
for you ...'

The lake – deceptive – wide-necked
and marsh ridden, had been traversed
by Lasseter without second thought –
but what of the boatman's charge?
And what of posterity claiming
that it had been Nebuchadnezzar
moonlighting as the Charon of Centralia?

Of Lightning Deflected from Rocks
to Nebuchadnezzar and Sheep

That the vapour,
stuff of lightning,
rose up out of its
cauldron – eyes bulging,
consuming all with cavernous,
electric breath, static rustling
the coarse hair of their bodies,
the appendages drawn in the shock,
feet strewn over rocky ground –
pinioning the torn body
that lifts to this heavenly
arc of blue o so blue,
the lightning unlocked,
the mechanism of forest
simulating the energy
of the wiry horns, the energy
of lightning collected
in the straggled locks
of a persistent sheep,
unkempt Nebuchadnezzar.

Silhouettes from a Fiery Furnace

I

Tri-faced
triptych of body
and resolution

'fell fast bound
into the heart of fires'

to and fro
the bitumen flame
– napalm –
ripening on contact
with the dwellers
of the furnace

to and fro
the flames
encouraging
embellishing
the grim faced,
almost resisting.

All fed Nebuchadnezzar's pain.

The clouds that cloaked the body
as it crossed the fringe of Paradise –
the beast assumed in sand and grass,
wanting no more than an allotted space,
and yet still possessed...divinely.

II

Avoiding the solid,
looking to reflection,
he traced spirals
in the clouds,
coloured the blank
rings of the moon.

Failing to link
humility with learning,
his necromancy fallen short,
he became as the pulse eaters,
though still lusting
after the equivocations
of human passion and speech.

The shadows
of a desert furnace,
of the apostate couriers
of inner heat,
of night parrots
wailing in the core.

Nebuchadnezzar Runs from the Hunters

That they pursued themselves,
that they took pot-shots
at no more than a flash of life –
the lion roaring at their heels,
encouraging the leather-hearted.
And that they hooted, shouted,
and cheered, in their chase,
bringing early warning to stars,
who tightened and held Nebuchadnezzar –
not for hunters to be free
amongst stars.

Nebuchadnezzar Views a Colonisation

His flame dulled aqua
the sharpened edge of rock,
the pinnacles of desert.

They'd come prepared –
he'd give them that –
though having long acclimatised
he remained confident
of preventing permanent
occupation ... running
indelible fire out over
the bursting sand,
exploding each particle –
mica, quartz, schist,
raging amongst the flame.

And that the brightness
brought hands to eyes,
that hearts and minds
froze over in veils.

And let it be known,
that so ruthless
did Nebuchadnezzar become
that he erased all trace,
right down to the grist
of their spirits.

The Golden Cancer

The cancer ran
St Elmo's fire
from the skerries
of Amadeus

the cancer ran
tempting

the lavatic mud
instantly dust

and Nebuchadnezzar
reaper of sand
blowing hot and cold

bristled and bubbled
like a disconsolate empire
in its manic death-throes.

Rain Passes Dominion to Starry Night.
White Nebuchadnezzar and White Dog
Discuss the Darkness Surrounding Stars

The liquid bouquet,
pot-pourri of dog star
humanising the delicate
features of beastliness,
viewed entirely from
the sprouted spine
of Nebuchadnezzar.

Translucent, these eruptions
mock the blank tableau of sky
until all become flowers
and the star consumes the eye.

From the weight of self –
the beast in Nebuchadnezzar's
every step – White Dog learnt
of a possible return.

Cloche-eyed, orbicular,
turning an indefinite tightness,
the dog star darkly brightens,
accelerates the aspirations
of star-gazers in its paradox.
'Phenomena – extraordinary!'

And a blind Nebuchadnezzar
cherished the Dominion of Heaven,
and ignored its persistent savagery.

Dialogue with St Antony

NEBUCHADNEZZAR: My back is now red and sphacelate,
the crows gnaw the slivers of my eyes.

ST ANTONY: And the forest has petrified,
and has become the dust of this
desert hellscape, and our lust
rages – simooms inciting fire.

NEBUCHADNEZZAR: When the will to resist weakens –
in sickness isolation pining –
the strength lies in preservation...

ST ANTONY: And I proclaimed my anger
and threatened my hunger
and still faith would not
leave me...

NEBUCHADNEZZAR: In the gnamma holes
water has become fire
and the night parrots
move gingerly in dusk light,
mocking with a small sadness,
their spirits rattling
spinifex prisons.

ESCHATOLOGIES
(1991)

THE MILLENARIAN'S DREAM

Inland

Inland: storm tides,
ghosts of a sheep weather
alert, the roads uncertain

families cutting the outback
gravel on Sunday mornings,
the old man plying the same track
to and from the session
those afternoons, evenings
(McHenry skidded into a thickset
mallee after a few too many
and was forced to sell up)

On the cusp of summer
an uncertain breeze
rises in grey wisps
over the stubble –
the days are ashen,
moods susceptible,
though it does not take
long to get back
into the swing of things

We take the only highroad
for miles as the centre
of the primum mobile – it's
the eye of the needle
through which our lives'
itineraries must be drawn,
a kind of stone theodolite
measuring our depths beyond
the straight and narrow,
it's a place of borrowed dreams
where the marks of the spirit
have been erased by dust –
the restless topsoil

Burnt Offerings

I *past*

We thought the whole town had gone up.
From the latticed balcony, the wormy woodwork
creaked as we leaned out further
trying to plumb the tangerine depths.
We caught only the moths flickering
on the edge of the burnt darkness.
                              Apparently,
somebody had pushed an armchair into an open fire.
Only one house had fallen to flame,
the rest to water.

II *present*

They say to go down early
if you want the best pickings,
the really dry wood. It's been
heaped up for months now,
though the wet has got into
it a bit – a furlike growth,
white on black skin, taking
over.
        And they say –
                          'If you're
into pyrotechnics, hang around, bring
a few beers down and watch while we pour
kero and petrol over the piles, the flameburst
sucking the air dry, throwing
rat and rabbit fireballs
in all directions...'

Rain-gauges

A triptych of rain-gauges
poised over a bore running
ten thousand of salt a day,
as dry as the lips of a pump
idle but for madness, pvc
pipes sweating though unable
to measure their ossification,
and time as brittle as the rings
of a smoked moon marking auras
like triumphs over the Dry & Damned,
the Wanderers, Measurers, Seekers
of Liquid, and those counting
the days since that Spring
morning when the decision
to settle had been taken.

Old Hands / New Tricks

A ring-necked parrot drops into flight,
fence posts collapse and ossify,
the wattle bird trims the lamp of wattle bloom

Despite storm weather the soaks diminish,
though by way of contrast the green tinge
of a late rain pokes its head over stubble –
the new growth that will yield no seed

About the homestead unripe fruit is severed
from trees – parrots jostle, making
swings and see-saws of their bodies

The wells are covered with railway sleepers
over-run with wire-weed and Mediterranean
Bugloss – Salvation Jane – which crisps over
cracks, gives cool water a taste of irony

In the pepper trees magpies threaten to unpick
the world as they know it – their songs are not
characteristic – old hands have learnt new tricks

Two Days Before Harvest

An easterly stretches and compresses
the deadwood fissures, strings of parakeets
arrange themselves into nets to drag
the breeze – their feathers firing,
the sun striking the afternoon pink.

In the soon-to-be-lopped heads of wheat
there burns the fidelity of summer – beyond,
on the white-bake of salt, lines of supply
are thinning and the dust of scuffed patches
drinks the blood of eucalypts. Topknot pigeons
encounter themselves, much to their surprise,
in foray from she-oak to powerline and back again.

The tines of a discarded scarifier have set
like the roots of trees ringbarked from memory –
you see, the tractor's welter, the jiggering
blades of the header, the crows teasing
the gate-posts, unlock a continuity
that would persist, or threaten to ...

The Compression of Time, Place and Incident

Fixed firmly, this comes as landfill,
a sealing of a tomb, a carving
of an epitaph. Too many times
I have sought the first notes
of a tune, the words of a song,
that would break the charm
that's held me to the farmer's words –
'Eagle, I'd remake you if I could.'
    At Wind's Crossing and Eagle Point,
tethered to that ghost known locally
as Hathaways, the farmer stirs
his ti-tree fires and casts iron
loops about the hoop of a wheel,
marks time with a bronze quill,
explores the sound lapse,
insists that somewhere the eagle
is trying to call – landlocked –
unable to reach its eyrie perched
high overhead on the outstretched
arm of a charred York gum,
at the centre of Achilles' shield.

Spontaneous Regeneration

I am here to rekindle
the moon dying in its race
for the sun, to break
the puff and bubble of salt,
to entertain the legions
of black-winged stilts
in their long march
to the dam, to harness
the wind dusting
knucklebones of a frayed

and peeling earth, to enter
the season of spontaneous
regeneration
                    in company.

Foxes and Python

A fox skin
in a nitrate bath,
and a fox skin drying
stiff as a card
folded over the levers
of a veteran plough,
stare fixedly at a python
coiled about the lintel
of the sheep shed – 'comes
down about once a month
for a feed', the farmer says,
pleased that it remains,
having appeared, like the foxes,
'out of the blue one day'.

Three-in-One Parable

The old fox looks into
the sky which is wider here
than anywhere, while the hunters
sing with their fox whistles
the Song of Asking.

During the day warm spots
settle in the fold of hill,
at night cold winds funnel
deep into the dreams of sheep.

Wells

I

The wire takes hold and spins in the hands,
severing shirt buttons. They pierce the dry
surface and tap clean water ten metres down,
the stigmata of the rough edges brought
through faith in an old timer's electricity.
Or maybe success is merely an aspect of faith,
that if the diviner is a brother or uncle
then you've got to believe in him. Waterwitching
slakes a thirst, greens the garden in places
where Summer forbids this abomination. Though
prayers of affirmation are required to keep
the water flowing – the Underworld has its
limitations and will bleed to death eventually.

II

Funnelling down to the source –
with a deep well a canvas fly directs
clean air to the digging – then angling
dry-stone walls or timbering with jamb posts.
The windlass moves the buckets up and down
simultaneously, meeting somewhere near
centre, though feigning balance. Working
the soft earth you'd wonder how water
could flow anywhere, though hitting rock
you'd wonder how it could ever change its course.
Looking up, the fly is full-blown with light,
the edges of the well are dark lines. The eyes
find it hard to adjust. Sometimes you remember
things like this when the well turns salt.

III

When the water turns salt, changes course,
or evaporates, they fill the hole with rubbish
from the house, paddocks, and sheds. Cavities
will usually form, making it a dangerous place
to explore. Edges crumble, cave-ins are common,

most often it is fenced off. Sometimes in
the search for a new source, the diviner will
track the ghost of water through its old course
and come to the plugged-up well. Refusing
to believe it possible, though unable to curb
their curiosity, more often than not farmers will
have the old well tested. The look on their faces
when they are told the water is clean and plentiful!

When I Go Alone

I

When I go alone
through the trill of stubble
into the salt
I do so
not in the moment
but in memory surveyed and charted
in some softer place.

Saltweed
ropes at my ankles,
erosion
channels my feet
and breaks each particle
away from its platform –
a flight of mountain ducks
erupts from the dam.

II

A modicum of Self
will outgrow its best intention – the magpies swagger
and are full of mourning, would seem to gloat,
would tear intruders apart, it is not their end
on which they're brooding: this is nesting season.

III

In the gnarled gullies
of Two People's Bay
the noisy scrub bird
builds its song
to the point of bursting,
not for human ears
it will cut the skin of the drum,
a sharp sound made empty.

I have skirted its territory as a child
unwittingly,
a cousin has tracked its song,
though none I know
has seen it / it has been said
      that on rare occasions
        it will mimic
      a human call for help,
        of joy.

IV

At canopy level
crossing a swing bridge
that floats on tension
I note the crumbling banks
the diminishing river
and catch the sensual patter
of thinning water, a voyeur
with a squint...

V

When I go alone
I accept that only animals
have souls and I must
court their blessings.

The magic
is in the naming –
though who's to trust
these guides and dictionaries?

Surely the name a creature
gives itself is spoken privately –
amongst its kindred, at a territorial
meeting, before setting out
on a migratory passage?

Maybe
all Namings are imminent –
that all shall be said
in the moment intervention
is accepted.

The Myth of the Grave

I

A pair of painted quails
scurries across the quills of stubble
a flurry of rapid
eye movement

they shadow my walk
ostentatiously
lifting and dropping
into invisible alleyways

reaching the grave
I turn to catch them

curving back, stopped
by the windrows

the grave is a magnet
that switches polarity
when you reach it.

II

The epitaph is measured
by the size of the plaque,
or is it the plaque that's
measured by the epitaph?

It seems to matter.
Death becomes a question
of economy – the lavish are big
on ceremony, slight on prayer.

III

At a distance
sheep leave salt-licks
beside a dam and zig-zag
down towards the shade.

Grey gums bend with the tide
of the breeze, the midday sun
would carry their doubles
to the grave and fill the urns.

The ground dries and crumbles,
a lizard darts out of a crack
and races across the paddock.
Do ashes rest easily here?

IV

A fresh grave that holds three
generations is something you question
on a first encounter. How in life
would they have felt about sharing

a single room in a shoebox flat?
Maybe, at an instant, only one soul
is resident, the others entering the bodies
of quails, exploring the wastes of stubble.

Voices from a Region of Extraction

MINER

Old Tin Lizzie
was the first car
in Kookynie – the fella
owed me money and wanted me
to take it in payment,
the kids pestering
and me understanding
that most of all they wanted
to be the first kids in town,
for a little while at least.

I told them we couldn't
afford to run it ...

MINER'S WIFE

From Perth to Woorooloo
the train wheezed and rasped,
clanked and jostled.

The sanatorium opened
on one side to allow
fresh air, protected
by no more than blinds
during storm weather,
which the men who couldn't
garden contemplated
opening and closing.

The chill morning air
would bite like razors
into their collapsing chests.
This was the open-air treatment.

The children, arms laden
with flowers grown in rich soil,
played at their feet,
and they harboured no bitterness.

MINER

Despite a dozen hotels
I would continue past all, straight
to the coffee palace with its wood
and whitewashed hessian walls.

I was happiest when working the Cosmopolitan,
it being in the middle of the town
and not much travelling.

And the war stripped the district
clean to the bone,
and the few mines left open
worked frantically.

MINER'S WIFE

I mean, he had to tell them himself
really, didn't he?

From Woorooloo to Perth
the train clanked and jostled,
wheezed and rasped
in tireless travel ...

MINER

She tells me the eldest
is working as a seamstress
and can no longer visit
on weekends.

I get them to bring me
the newspapers ... I read
year after year
of the continuing boom.

They came once, the photographers
from the newspaper – the city newspaper –
and had us all sitting there: bleached, dry,
though liquid faced.

MINER'S WIFE

And then I caught the boy
floating in the red creek
in an old rainwater tank,
though I left him to it,
it not having rained
for months.

And I said that if my church isn't good enough,
then I'll be damned if I'll go into hers.

And I left water
on the verandah
for the wanderers
of the desert
and respected
the spirits.

MINER

Once lost in the desert
it becomes the fullest memory.

Where those who weary
of their clothes
scream for cover
in the hours before sunrise.

The red desert,
where every particle
howls ...

Afghans came in the end.
On camels ... with their clocks,
boxes, and scented furniture.
They gave me water.
The town was almost dry.

His lips were blue.
I've barely room for this.
And to find a place for it
in this household of a brain
I've been left with after
years of shuffling our lives.
Ah, his feet so cold
his eyes glazed and receding,
his lips ... cornflowers.

Pillars of Salt

We always look back,
attracted by that feeling
of having been there before – the roads
sinking, the soil weeping (scab on scab
lifted), fences sunk to gullies
catching the garbage of paddocks,
strainers blocked by stubble
and machinery and the rungs
of collapsed rainwater tanks / and maybe
the chimney and fireplace
of a corroded farmhouse, once
the guts of the storm, now
a salty trinket.

The salt is a frozen waste
in a place too hot for its own good,
it is the burnt-out core of earth's eye,
the excess of white blood cells.
The ball-and-chain rides lushly
over its polishing surface, even dead wood
whittles itself out of the picture.

Salt crunches like sugar-glass, the sheets
lifting on the soles of shoes (thongs scatter
pieces beyond the hope of repair) – finches
and flies quibble on the thick fingers
of salt bushes, a dugite spits
blood into the brine.

An airforce trainer jet appears,
the mantis pilot – dark eyed and wire
jawed – sets sight on the white wastes
for a strafing run: diving, pulling out
abruptly, refusing to consummate.

                                    Salt
explodes silently, with the animation
of an inorganic life, a sheep's skull no more
than its signature, refugees already
climbing towards the sun
on pillars of salt.

The Millenarian's Dream

I

On the Glad Day the sheep
penned themselves and offered
their wool willingly.
An old shearer was seen standing
on an outcrop of quartz down
by the 'thousand acre' paddock.
At the pub that night somebody
said he'd been on fire. The old
shearer denied it, saying
it must have been the sunset.

II

The sky's props popped and crackled
as they struggled to hold their burden,
even ghosts moved en-masse out of the mulga
to witness what promised to be a holocaust.

III

The five-pointed flower
struggled to outgrow
                outshine
the darkest polypus: the spent tin mine
they'd blocked with a few sticks
of gelignite after a couple of kids
had fallen in and perished

the crows spreading
as the heat peeled
the layers of sight.

IV

Intaglioed on the silo walls
the cat and its litter inflected
the bloodier face of wheat: ASW,
Australian Standard White.

They hooted and cheered
in the pub that night, washing
it down straight from the tap,
while in the limelight

a stranger had sat, marking
dust and twisting a glass,
clenching a fist, wiping
rust from his lips.

V

These are only a few of the many images
that came to mind as cosmonauts 999 Days
and 1000 Days watched Mother Earth shade
herself like a child's etch-a-sketch.

The sun, caught in the child's decline
refused to rise, while the larks
fired between the cosmonauts' eyes,
outspun the concentric layers of sight.

Counterfeit

Lasseter
knew the will-o-the-wisp
to be no more
than freedom's counterfeit

from the heart
of conflagration
he knew

from the core
of reef
he knew

and the will-o-the-wisp
loved him for this.

Photism

It wasn't gold
but girasol

And though beautiful
in its own right

Perceptual and spilling fire
the miners unsettled

The bones of Lasseter,
ground the spirits

Of the place to dust
and squeezed tight

The earthplates.
Need it be said

The girasol wept
tears of blood.

The Shedding

The mulga ghost
skirts its thinning shores

Sings its impenetrable centre –
richer than this atmosphere

Of gold dust and a bloodshot iris.
Light-footed under heavy skies

It barely activates Daniel's
second half – cryptaesthesia

A slow-moving bird whose territory
stretches no further than the tomb

Of reef, a grey or even green blur
on the frame of the photograph.

Every boom or bust story
has its boundaries, and even

Prophets fail to predict the precise
time of a shedding.

CATCHMENT

Catchment

I *zone*

In a catchment zone the keepers
must keep clean houses, sweeping
soot from the roots, scouring
granite outcrops regularly.

The catchment's focus – a saline pool,
comfortable in its illusion of deep, clear water –
sheds itself in the stubs of severed trees
hedging the waterline.

II *quarry*

Examining the dross of a quarry,
(the coarse and fine sizes), we may grasp
what it is that has reduced things to this:

the panorama sliced away in cross section,
exposing the roots in their bed of rock;
or in the deeper layers, the mechanism driving
the rust of ironface, feeding the surface's scrub,
slipped buttresses, cliff faces...
                              the risk of overextension
threatening the pristine catchment:
the quarry top seeking to cover the wounds.

III *pipes and valves*

We scale the wall, rising up over the filaments
of pumping station – pipes, straitjacketed,
annelids splitting and regenerating in and out
of the slinking earth, skirting the valley,

entwining undergrowth
                    the valves feeding
from their concrete outriggers (weir-houses
inhabited by pressure gauges, clacks, and screws),
their task reason enough for existence, thoughts
on source and destination not one of their strong points.

IV *the wider waters*

Sloughs of mosquitoes squeezing in and out
of sluices in a hillside cast barely
a collective shadow over the catchment.

At the foot of a spillway, past seasons
wallow in brackish puddles, raft insects
eke out sketchy existences
                    thin lines of pines
cling to retainer walls.

From the summit – the barrier neither moulded nor bound
by roots, but soldered to the squared shoulders
of valley – we look to the liquid centre: wind slicks
flattening the ripples, ironing them out, wiping
the corrugated glass clean, darning patches
on the wider waters.

At the Serpentine Pipehead

Defrocked camellias,
their discarded skirts
rotting in unceremonious heaps –
*The Water Board hopes you have
enjoyed your visit, welcomes
suggestions* – I suggest the plum flower,
the almond blossom...I suggest the song
of a lorikeet cast like a net
through the deadwood of spent trees,

I suggest the area closed off
because of dangerous chemicals,
I suggest the solitary catboat,
its limp sail a premonition,
a marooned pilotless ferry
on the distant bank.

Crossing the wall of the small pipehead
a child crouches to view the waters,
through the space between fence
and concrete – the green mesh confusing
the picture, preventing pure vision.
I trace the lime-sweat tributaries:
spread like bruised capillaries
they broach the hairline cracks of the walkway.
I admire the lichen welding the walls:
no talus-creep, these rocks have fallen neatly
into place, though the position of hills
and filtered river is by chance.

Metaxu

I *Patterson's Curse / Salvation Jane*

It's what you do when the chips are down,
or when transport and a few hours
present themselves – passing the overflow
of Patterson's Curse   (spillage riding the firebreaks
                        deep down the slopes, sloshing
                        at the walls of the saddle dam,
                        double sown at the edge of road,
                        embroidered by stock ...)
                                    The wattle & daub
of the catchment's absorbent surface – the jarrah
and bracken ferns, wildflowers and lemon-scented gums
(with blackened bases like the termite-free power poles
of suburban streets), the magnified credulity
of a patch of skin.

Internal vibration to compact cement –
though, as usual, I place my hands to sense the warmth
that movement brings and find none greater
than that reflected from the spread of curiosity.
                                                                Unseen,
the tunnel forms the true bridge, though it's hard
to come to grips with this when you're sailing the perfect
course of the wall: between water and air, blue sky
and dark rock, heavy clouds and a glimpse of a would-be
phosphorescence in the heart of the waters.
                                                    Though the tunnel
carries more than implications of a saturated life:
                                                            granite
& dolerite dykes rock-bolted, slabbed to the floor of a vast
building that has as its roof the floor of the catchment;
and maybe the core of that purple encroachment –
                                                        Salvation Jane.

II   *Filters*

Filters – you set them up to prevent the truth
with its rough-hewn aggregate crushing you down
and damming the flood – you quote purity – maybe
silently, but letting it creep into gestures,
a lack of patience – you can feel the tension
in the wall. As you sit on a granite outcrop
looking up at the dark face, an aspect of seepage
(from the galleries your scream of 'Watch out!
It's going to burst!' can only be heard by
other inspectors) will traverse the interlock
of tightened space as easily as rain shatters
the prospect of a leisurely walk through
the catchment (Jarrah Dieback – you are near
a Forest Disease Risk Area: Quarantine   Horse
or Vehicle is Prohibited) and sickness is a monolith
movable only by sound mechanics.
                                        Leakage paths are woven
by frogs, the flight paths of crow and cockatoo,
the crack and regurgitation of warblers, the bantering
of 28s ... They mark time, we count our steps back
to transport, we do not risk holding hands, an embrace –
we are treading water, the taps carry rust

preserved in the wall-crack, history turned
in the crusher barrels, the size greater than its gauge,
the tension no longer filtered ... our love percolates,
is filtered in its own making, is the seepage
that defies the walls, attempts to bridge the gap.

Stretching the Vista

A strelitzia parts the folds
of humidity with its beak
of cartilage – but don't be fooled,
it's just held out against
the year's last frosts,
and its foliage flexes confidence.
The risk here is to be channelled
into a particular vista, that caught
in the concrete spillway
you may fail to realise
that a bird of paradise
will fly unnoticed in this unfamiliar
territory – where blue-green water
spreads wide to its sienna rim,
makes islands and bottlenecks
of land look luxuriant.
Stretching the vista in all directions
a bearded dragon zig-zags
over the dam's drier face,
a clockwork ziggurat restrains
a tense silence – white horses
warm to a desert wind and swim
against the anchored points
of a tourist compass. The lack
of overflow teases the laden clouds
without making them spill their hearts,
the wind continues its seduction
in playing the jarrah strings
of the catchment lyre,
the pink flute of erosion.

Pipeline

The pipeline cleaves the catchment
with its good intention – on a watersling
outflowing the silver jacket, palmed
off by pumping station after pumping
station, though losing none of its spring,
darting forwards with a hop, skip, and a jump
riding sidecar to a national highway,
swinging from one climate to another
without a change of expression.
                              An egret flies
lower over a coastal reservoir, parrots
in unclaimed territory know the pipeline
to be a hot cable that will burn through claw,
a crow senses moisture at the final
pumping station.
                    In passing, it remains
indifferent to farm machinery, to the crisp
and wink of saltpans, to finches tossing
their hoods back and tittering
about its stiff shell.
                        In passing, it gloats inwardly
before leaving a dry wind that's been shooting
its skin to wrestle with scrub, before plunging
head first into red earth.

Victoria Dam

Crossing the spillway, contrary
to the line of flow, casting
back over the dross, slicing
banks, drainage, liquid
tailings, you find the shoulder –
dam wall curving away,
like a rock on a string,

car accelerating into a corner,
tension dragging it in.

The sun sinks into the socket
of valley, an eye nerved
with green blood of canopy
covering the escape
or evacuation of fresh and stale
water mingled. Powerlines coaxing
overhead, though indifferent
to the mud up to your ankles.

Escorted and then abandoned
to the mechanics of the poem,
you cable echoes, ringing
out of the damp basin on
tenuous rungs of shadow.
White-trunked sentinels
stare bemused – so, this
is what's at the bottom of it!

The rough and the smooth
face of the spillway wall – the dry
as smooth as glass, the wet
rough, lime-leached, disconsolate,
despite its extra skin (blood
had crept up and sourced new veins).

        The basin flicks
the wind up as you stand on the lip
of spillway, sifting a birdcall
unrecognised. Below, scabs form
over an emptied heart, a desert
walled by forest.

Vehicles congest on the far abutment –
like a wake they laugh, come maybe
for the felling, breath spent,
marking out their takings. You notice
prints of track-driven machinery
set in cement near the base of wall.
An engineer considers the dam –

'Water leaching through the wall
has sucked lime out of the matrix –
the concrete is crumbling,
the iron inside is rusting
and an explosion is possible,
even a tremor could set
the whole thing off.' Ti-tree
has lanced its roots deep, clutching
aggregate, distorting flow tests.

From White Gates up to Old Victoria,
then to tanks in Kalamunda, Lesmurdie,
Walliston, and Bickley, water swinging
its way up and out of the catchment.
The ranger sings, 'It's the rhythm
you want, the rhythm of White Gates
and Old Victoria.' He says the cement
that holds the walls was shipped by clipper
from England, that if it was left
another year it would reach a hundred.
Though he has to admit, you could take
a shower by standing beneath the leaks.

In the half-light an engineer
takes stock and sight of the white-boxed
seismic recorder, climate station,
survey pillars – he wanders towards
the marker flags, forerunners
of the new dam. 'Dam engineers
talk of downstream, drainage
engineers talk upstream,' he laughs.
His arms arc through forest.
When the old dam was drained
birds came in waves and picked
reef on reef of freshwater mussels
left stranded. Siphoned,
the flesh-centred aggregate
bleeds as the moon dominates,
as we make our way up or down stream.

Retired Reservoir

A cleft between hills stripped
to gravel and black granite, brief
stands of jarrah and gums heavily scarred,
a thin wall etched with seepage's motif.

I stand on high ground and glance
down onto the wall, its rocky shoulder
soothed by overflow, the comfort of white water,
an unseen creek below gathering confidence.

Rain cuts up through the valley
and thuds against the pitted face,
which disappears, cut off by the testimony
of birdcall. Clouds clot on a precipice.

I cannot take the many paths towards
the valley's centre – their surfaces
are temporary, while mere thought erodes,
and birdcall cuts water's salient devices.

PLUMBURST

The Orchardist

Orange trees cling
to the tin walls
of his home. A red
checked shirt and grey
pair of trousers hang
over the one-eyed tractor.
His oranges are small suns
and he is an astronaut
floating slowly
through their spheres
of influence.

The Orchard

1

It is not my place, though he seeks
to make it this. Overcome by the city
it is in need of defence. I think he would like
a gang of strong arms to protect against the gangs
of his delusions, to ward off the organised,
the planned attrition. I offer words, and in hard times
these are almost enough. I speak to truants,
warning them off, apologising for a scared
old man threatening with his pitchfork.

2

Seen from the heart of the picking – astride
the gridwork of trees – the vacancies are voids
through which predators and visitors will plot
their course. In itself, this is as it should be,
but something doesn't fit into the picture
of 'paths coincident on being anon twin halves
of one august event', or maybe this is a puzzle
of material, labour, and event, from which some vital
piece is missing, or has been overlooked.

A Field of White Butterflies

There is a lot of mystery in me…
he explains, peering deep into my eyes.
As a child I would examine the smallest
things, things that would not ordinarily
be seen. My mother would tell the neighbours
that I was a daydreamer, there was no other way
of explaining it. That was in a very
cold place, high in the mountains
above Dalmatia in Yugoslavia.
I came here when I was eighteen
looking for work. I knew about
the languages of animals and plants.

Three seasons ago you couldn't
look at this paddock without seeing
a white butterfly – consuming, crowding
even themselves out of existence.
Last season I saw two, two white butterflies
in the whole year. This year the Monarch
will come, mark my words – wandering
down over the hills, settling
pince-nez on the potato flowers.
You see, where people settle
imbalance follows, the air
being full of white butterflies,
or there being no white butterflies at all.

Ibis

An ibis picks between thin veins
of grass surfacing on open ground,
recently upturned, nourished in mist
and exhumed by the morning sun.

Stilt-legged it stalks on a pivot,
graceful in its geometrics.
It is difficult to pinpoint
the centre of balance,
which imparts a life of its own.

In flight it lunges slowly
as though it were not meant
to be airborne, its legs
tight outriggers, mouthpiece
a curved pipette
drawing and discharging
the grey-blue sky.

I also remain afloat
– an ibis – riding the crests
and troughs of a changing surface,
settling on aspects of thought,
treading lightly the outskirts.

Ibis Myth

Ibises fan out over
a paddock next to an arterial road
welling under the residue of rains,
and work their black beaks
systematically. We move with them.

Should the scene be brightened
by ignoring the houses, powerlines,
fuel leaking from a petrol station?
Ibises are precise in their scansion.
Not a brief glimpse, we must consider,
that interpretation comes later – the image
consumes the sullen plains, the flock
will fly (in Grace). Stretching
from centre to extremity,
the myth accounts
for the adaptable...the one straw-necked ibis
                                    moves freely with nine
                                    of the sacred variety.

On Albert Tucker's *Ibis in Swamp*

What action prevails
in the miasma of swamp?
The mummified ibis reflects – reflected
in the crescent of its black moon beak.
Life almost crisp amongst decay
makes decay necessary
                                    even muted flowers
become profoundly
beautiful.
                Sacred Ibis
wades green light
thick with shadows, the stilled eye
accepts the dark heart welling
in its hollowed log.

The Essence of Camellias

*The essence of created things
is to be intermediaries.*
SIMONE WEIL

Past their moment
Citizens
   of a bruised empire
 an imperial red
     crushed under,
That not even
    the naivety
Of a Rousseau
    could capture.
Beneath the glossed sun
     of memory
Rosettes vitrify,
    their essence
Mimicking
   the created shape.

Camellias, prima donnas
    of the pyrotechnic,
Their dance floor
    humus black.

Paperbarks

Paperbarks scream out of childhood
deep into wetlands – lightning, a silver flash
of the fringe, though as subliminal as ghosts,
their territory that of the spirit.
Water fallen, dank goitres tease
our thirst, skins peel and flake
about the grasping roots, sweltering

in the red tinge of earth. Though holding light
absorbent skins will not extinguish when voice
falls and memory lingers, for these are ghosts
who sing the stagnant weathers,
and brew storms out of drought.

The Bottlebrush Flowers

A Council-approved replacement
for box trees along the verges
of suburban roads, it embarrasses
with its too sudden blush – stunning
at first, then a burning reminder
of something you'd rather forget.
And it unclothes so ungraciously –
its semi-clad, mangy, slovenly,
first-thing-in-the-morning appearance.
And while I've heard it called
a bristling firelick, a spiral
of Southern Lights, I've also seen
honey-eaters bob upside down
and unpick its light in seconds.

Plumburst
(for Wendy)

The neat greens of Monument Hill
roll into sea, over the rise the soft rain
of plumfall deceives us in its groundburst.

If lightning strikes from the ground up,
and Heaven is but an irritation that prompts
its angry spark, then plums are born
dishevelled on the ground and rise
towards perfection...

Out of the range of rising plums
we mark the territory of the garden,
testing caprock with Judas trees,
pacing out melon runs. Behind us a block
of flats hums into dusk and the sun
bursts a plum mid-flight.

Windows

I

You follow the smoke-column
from a garden fire to a point
near the top of the window
where it liaises with the dark
waste of clouds. From the ash,
still warm, the bulbs – electric –
throw off their shucks.

II

The wind stirs a vague notion
from its frame – the sweep
of the Sleepy Mallow of Peru,
the shimmering Arizona Cypress,
the hillocked paddocks,
the cankered orchard,
the errant hawk riding the boundaries,
and a fell moon straining to claw
the inhabitants of a dark room
out into the finest of days.

STRANGE METAPHORS

Dry Dock Sculpture

On the mantelpiece
a Giacometti
sits in company
just as is,
holding itself well,
a stretched body
standing up
to the decay
of a damask rose
in miniature vase –
a Giacometti
on the mantelpiece –
an earthbound figurehead,
a vessel without sails.

Kenneth Noland's *A Warm Sound in a Gray Field, 1963*

A warm sound in a gray field
finds it may break out consistently,
letting the breath of discovery
flow in rings spread warmly
out over a gray field.

The bell chime – love's corona –
feeds back into itself,
through all landscapes,
a variety of atmospheres,
trembling imperceptibly
at the centre.

There is a point where tensions
grip the heart, where darkness
seeks a glimpse; though all is quiet
as a warm sound in a gray field
steps in to play its part.

the insulation of the new york sonnet
(for Noel Sheridan)

I don't know if there's such a thing
as the new york sonnet, and I can't find
out until I get my copy of Denby back
from a guy who shot through to Carnarvon
at short notice. It's not likely that
tracking stations, bananas, racism, and
the Gascoyne River are going to yield
a response, but Denby, to whom you handed
a cup of tears some years ago in a film
that was rumoured to be a sonnet in itself,
holds the answer, not so much in the dance
of language, but in his collecting insulators
from the tops of power pylons and giving them
as tokens of gratitude to his closest friends.

Dissolving

Those gods made permanent by photochemistry
rise dripping from the tanks of inky fluids,
rehearsing their tricks of significance
JOHN TRANTER

In the one solution any number of images
will be dissolving simultaneously;
take this short from a soon-to-be-released
film: the dealer moves into a free
transit zone, packing an electric drill
and looking like a powder monkey, the wind
licks the bowl of the river and sings
a ditty that goes something like this – *and*
those who ping speed, whack smack, hit coke,
blat angel dust, cook acid, will taste
anything that gives a rush. The flesh
squabbles about the anode and cathode
of its own solution, while people from
the censorship board note where each
particle travels, how long it takes to disperse
and congregate. Charged by the cut and thrust
of expectation, travelling the frescoed
halls and filling the pink stucco rooms
of the script, you forget that interval
is a small drama in itself – that maybe
the sappers working at the base of the bridge
have a lot to do with the dissolving storyline,
that the zodiac bobbing lightly will take
photographers, sound mixers, seagulls,
and the train passing overhead, out
of the picture before you've had a chance
to get back into the theatre for the second
half, before that drug dealer has dissolved
the drug, filled your electric veins.

Eschatology

Best left unsaid. Reflect the day
the earth stood still. Consider.

You collect partitions. Meteor trains
tubing their cold way through space.

And the desert is the same. Partitions.
Sub-divisions split from the soul.

Too much the cold months on all planets.
Too much.   Fromm's

death cantos roll on arcanely,
parodying their binding. In desert

the structure of our fortune
can be examined in the sand's snaking,

the vicissitude of starlight,
the realignment of body fluids.

Heaven's flat green fields welding
the globe. Partitioned from space.

Strange Metaphors

> *'Isn't he the guy who uses strange metaphors –*
> *like describing cars with teeth?'*
> ANTHONY LAWRENCE

Collapse is wild with symmetry
and mechanical savants move with artistic
hands – making poetry out of the angry
expressions of car grilles. The drinks
waiter steps in just in the nick of time

and offers a vision of a sturgeon sailing
through flaccid waters driven by an ambient
wind, getting no further than the length
of its entrails. The clean-shaven makes
a cameo appearance, the grey barrel suit
setting the forget-me-not off perfectly.
After all, we are poets, and have got to be
able to make sense of this. Look! Quickly
the wedge-tailed eagle takes leave of its
broken body – no time to waste, it's a long flight
back to the Nullarbor. And, great joy, the day
is ours – watch Ashbery dip into a hint of Rilke
and lodge himself delicately amongst our words.
Though let's be wary and not display the trophy
yet – somebody at a distant table is suggesting
that there's more than a hint of ghost writer
about this, that strange metaphors have been
forced to do their captor's bidding.

The James Dickey Poems

Divining James Dickey

The pages flit about the binding.
Water witching my fingers idle words
on waters of Braille. Chosen
carefully it reads: *Now in the last
stand of wheat they bend* and   as
if to increase the odds   *For under
the mild white sun*. Stretching.
Ewes with six kilos of wool on their backs
clean their arses on a blowtorch.

Divining brings motive into question.
A complacence that lumps Fate
on its victims, soothed under the mild
white sun, bending with words tight
to the pasture, enmeshed in wheat.

the music

James Dickey comes back to me
under the Norfolk pine trees –

I am the *sweet flesh* he'd enjoy
hunting, flaying and splaying

as a trophy, a notch on the 3D
screen of poetry, the distillation

of a prayer. You too are of this flesh,
as are the tracks left by a bear

or bison, the droppings of a wild turkey.
James Dickey comes back to me

under the Norfolk pine trees,
his blade probing its skin, its hair.

the flawed imperative

The page moves with
the knife-blow of the pen,
the zipper of an anorak
clicks slowly, driven against
a cold that would make metal
brittle, seize the mechanism,
no matter how simple.
                    Cold air,
held tight to the chest,
the warmth of two bodies pressed
close together replicated,
our love is always distant,
and absent when forest
closes over – day's end.
                    Take
the mountain path, avoid the lower
ground – you should write this also,
if you can anchor the page

to the scent of animals
turning in their graves, on the surface.
Nearing a road, the outskirts
of a town – timber country,
an axe swings and rings
you to its blow, the iron
meridian bracing flesh
to bones. And thinking – now!
Seize the moment! Take aim
blindly and loose your arrow,
discard the measured step,
the hunter's respect,
rend the ashen lake of dusk.

the moon, a thumbprint with hollowed veins

The moon, a thumbprint with hollowed veins
(marking the shining eye of the page), risks
extinction in courting an old woman's prayers,
for through her all aspirations are focussed,
concentrated; and should she be a poet,
or have had a poet lover in her youth,
the moon's danger would be double-enhanced.
But the moon cannot mark its thoughts indelible
on the jailor's page with a mere hot press
of its thumb, and a wolf at its feet will taste
only the scent of the jailor in its blood,
for its veins are thickly filled, and the hunter's
call (eyes pressed to the moon) marks the steel,
a thumbprint with hollowed veins, the page.

The Vegetable King

Taking the shape
Of the Vegetable King
Leaves little room for enjoying
What's offered to our bony
Hearts; I say, let him in, take

Fluid, skin, and fibre, and bind
Your flowing, let
Sight imbue blood
And shadow.
                    The Vegetable King
Sets nets to catch the fragments
Of our bodies, his maleness
A comfort, though careful
Where his hair-roots lead; saturnalia,
A turning of earth in every
Loamy cup that's spent
Ripening his crown or tuber –
And in his gratitude
Taking stock of what could be
If the weather were to turn,
Or his potency fail – reciting
Always, to the mother, the
Deus misereatur, growing
With the flow, from heart
To shadow, Heaven to grave.

The Rites of James Dickey

> *They fall, they are torn,*
> *They rise, they walk again.*
> > 'The Heaven of Animals'

Nothing lost, nothing gained,
Instinct or knowledge blind in pain;
A slow chair rocks on the edge
Of the forest, the herding
Of death and marriage – celebration
Bright in the brochures, lush
With a day's work spent like a wire's
Tension: sunrise suspended, ecstatic
Death rekindled, this the torn flesh
Preparing to rise and settle again.

They fall, they are torn,
They rise, they walk again.

Dark bones bleached in Heaven,
The arrow's tip as sharp
As inspiration's spark
As strong as wire, the arrow
A beak furrowing an already green
Surface. The forest unnaturally
Still – storm-waiting, lavishing
Silence on tension. Confused, animals
Walk new climates, localities, their
Habits complying no longer.

They fall, they are torn,
They rise, they walk again.

And sleepers are restless,
The pits of their Unknowing
Filled – light forcing the wound,
Blood nor flesh able to drive
It out. The singer, the maker
Of the sermon, feeling ground
Loosen, air grow thin, sky
Bellowing close to his skin,
His soul moving out towards
The Heaven of Animals.

fait accompli

Death performs
With the pain of accuracy –
What trees refuse
The flesh of stone
Absorbs – We the dancers
Empty handed,
Electric and fragile
On the tips
Of our toes.

To the tips
Of our fingers
We are expected to dance

The floor of canyons
Sun-white, though
As sharp as frost.
The body cramps,
Celebrations
End. The animal sun,
The animal moon,
Singing the hunter,
His emptied veins,
The music of sinew
and taut muscles,
Of the leap frozen
In sleep.

Parahelion Over Foreshore / By Extension

a red ball is held between the sun and its child,
a red ball is held between the sun and its child...

the child looks up and the red ball eclipses its parent,
the child looks up and the red ball eclipses its parent...

the sun burns the arm away that holds the red ball
twice over

       the arm gone the ball seems to float
       the arm gone the ball seems to float

twice over
the sun burns the arm away that holds the red ball
the corpses of blowfish strewn on the jetty's deck,
the corpses of blowfish strewn on the jetty's deck
disturb him / by extension...

          over the edge the sun smiles
          over the edge the sun smiles

an arm reaches out
an arm reaches out
      holding a red ball
      holding a red ball

the child looks up and the red ball eclipses its parent,
the corpses of blowfish strewn on the jetty's deck
disturb him/by extension...
      over the edge the sun smiles
      holding a red ball
      an arm reaches out,
A red ball is held between the sun and its child

mondrian / laboratory / mounting pedestals

the fume cupboards
that must accompany
stacks on the roof
of a laboratory
infuse the notion
that ibises
were manufactured
as prototype
Concorde airliners/
that Mondrian's *Starry
Sky above the Sea*
is the fracture
of luminosity's eloquence:
when stacks strive
for an art that becomes
the random discharge
of particles mounted
on a pedestal
in a room composed
of form's colourful
building blocks

Still Life /
Pavilion and Cherry

HOME   VISITORS
an empty oval
draws sight
to the bare pitch,
with more than a green tinge
it rolls itself flat,
a strip of film

the bowler
breaks the stumps
at the *river end*,
someone had shaped
to glance – blinded
by the sun reflecting
off the freshly painted
pavilion

some time back
a stranger was killed
in the outfield,
a cherry dropping
from the sky,
lost in the swirl
of lights, striking
head–on.

LILITH

The Ribs of Adam

The first Eve failed the adamtest –
how many ribs do I have? he asked.
She could not answer and faded
back into the dirt of Paradise.
The second Eve guessed right,
with a little help from the serpent,
who was not Baal but Lilith
on a Narcissus kick.

Libation

She poured thick red wine
from the cup over her stomach
and ran her fingers through it.
This is a libation for myself
she said, this is my self love
       this is my self hatred
       this is my defeatism
       this is my id floating
on a tide of my own blood,
this is a waste of perfectly
good wine.

A Centurion's Wife

Odd that an extra
member of *his* entourage
should raise her head
after so many years.
That not even the gnostics
had ventured to mention
this hanger-on, malingerer
who'd managed to install
herself in the sacred tomb.

That it was she who gathered
crumbs from under the table,
delivered loaves, consoled
lepers as sores re-opened.
That it was she who sought
life in the tree withered
in its failure to bear fruit,
returned coins, saved
fish from the nets.

The Machinist

I'm probably saying more than I should
when I bring to your mind those five women
in Picasso's *Les Demoiselles d'Avignon* – I am
the one on the top left, though looking a little
less angular now, age and life having rounded
my figure. So, here I am, in this far away
from anywhere country, in old age, mourning
my lostlife. Yes, I do have children, and no
I never married. Actually, my son died
not so long ago. Both daughters are married,
one to an artist whose paintings sell for anything.
Strange that you should come here and ask
about my life … has somebody identified me
from that painting? Did Picasso leave notes?

Notes on the Succuba

> *the sacred owl shall also rest there, and
> find for herself a place of rest*
> ISAIAH 34:14

Folding her wings
the succuba settles.

In this dream she rides
high above the earth,
refusing the recumbent position,
recycling her love.

          *

The Ineffable Name spoken
the nightjar dislodged darkness
made ash of the stars.

The averted face,
the seed that is blood,
the weeping that eats
at her offspring.

*

The city lights
are old childless women
she has left stranded.

When a child laughs
in its sleep
they flick its nose:
a charm against Lilith,
the ring about her neck.

But Lilith loves.
Lilith is the sunflower
tracking the sun.

*

the shape of the dance
is the shape of the journey
is the shape of waking
is the shape of conjecture
bursting out of itself

the shape of the music
is the shape of sight
is the shape of taste
is the shape of night
is the shape of the dance (of life)
lost to its own choreography,
    morphology

*

The seduction of dreaming?
How many lie with minds open
lusting after the vision (beautiful),
tempted by their own creation

And of Senoi, Sansenoi, and Sammangelof:
their rings are her prison.

*

the sacred owl
grown restless,
climate and circumstance
changing, sidewinds,
(broken winged)
across the darkening
sand

Lilith Secretes Herself in the Creation of a Nietzschean Aphorism

Standing in the garden
Nietzsche bent down, plucked
a flower, and held it to his nose.
In the act of picking this flower
Nietzsche lost track of Necessity,
or Necessity lost track of Nietzsche.
A voice whispered in his ear:
'You have succumbed to desire, my dear.'

Lilith on Renaissance Gardens

I *the trophies of marius*

From the 1499 edition
of the Hypnerotomachia Poliphili
we may glean a love of geometry,

Poliphilus, Dominican monk,
could not see past a dream
of love outstruggling the Island,
place of love's desiring.

The outer rings of cypress and myrtle
manicured hedges encircling all species
of nimble lovers   yearning & flowering
        or lazing in the sun

II *the dream garden's incarnation*

Cat thyme and rue, lavender cotton
        and Southernwood.
Germander and marjoram. A green peacock
drinking from a bowl or buried deep in a bed
        of love-lies-bleeding.

Lilith and the Minotaur

I *vitriol*

In the gown
of the seventh maiden

(Daedalus supplied the threads)

Lilith faced the Minotaur
confident that she
would be loved.

She warned of death
and said vitriol
would be his lament.

II *splice*

The Minotaur
drank Lilith's swelling heart
which would not be emptied

conscience spliced them together,
the Minotaur grew protective

the heart shrivelled,
and was emptied

III *release*

sympathy –
the mere thought
set her straight

she lured Theseus
to break this infatuation

she bled
a silver thread

Chimera Song

chimera calls the nightjar
sung double-faced in sun and shadow,
come together in old style on elder
ground expects Lilith to follow
    as it would itself

solicitous angels guard
their quarry well, not even chimera,
hidden at will, can nudge its way
through the bars and into her jail

chimera, watcher of the fluid Graces
take heart in what you gather –
the coldest whisper, the strainings
at Vespers, delight outbrooding
    a nightjar's flight

Arum Lily Songs

I

the confident centrepiece
quivers amongst the sheer
folds of its robes.

would you believe
death's mute obsession
speaks easy at night

or that bisque cupolas
turn into themselves
when placed indoors?

II

the arrangement of lilies
on the sainfoin-encrusted banks
is planned
            they do not open
wantonly, do not spill their seed
carelessly

III

an old lady cuts lilies
in the early morning

her skin bubbles
under a red rash

she fills her basket
for the cemetery

these are the offspring of Lilith,
the lily is her flower

Lilith Considers Two Who Have Died Young

Hart Crane

Keats had nothing on this one, he who hurled
and was hurled himself, he of the caustic waterfront
manner, singing songs by the wharves as the dead
drifted by. This one had a sweet tooth. And the ego was
there for the filling – I got to him once in a dentist's
chair and had him gloating over the prospect of genius,
of seventh heavens and seven spheres and wild dances
under the moon of aether, of arseholes on cold cell
floors, of suns rising and sinking beneath his feet,
of epic and graft, of a bottle of Mercurochrome
       that mapped a gut-wrenching elegy.

Sylvia Plath

She offered her father
though in truth he wasn't
up to it. She offered her
lovers, even her husband.
I'd taken them a long
time back. The children,
strangely she refused.
Not to say she turned
me down flat, but rather
equivocated to a point
where the evaporating
flesh lost voice.

Lilith and Gunabibi Agree on Territory

LILITH: So, mine will be of darkness
and interminable cold; or of fire
and white heat. You can take
the temporal ground.

GUNABIBI: I shall take the living. And I shall take
you should you choose a manifest life.
All are without time and dream the dream
I make them receptive to, though the dream
is not mine...

LILITH: And I shall be God's messenger,
if you like.

Lilith Speaks

The pensive and subliminal
the conscience delicately
flexing its muscles
toning down love
discreetly

that offspring leap from bodies
chaste, when love is no more than
apparatus, appendage, decoration
to the mechanics...

                driven to an altered state
I slide into sweet non life,
always myself,
always part of the moist kiss
that numbs

A Note

Great evening thought Lilith –
they fed on my anecdotes,
drank my self-effacements,
wiped their mouths
on my disasters ...
Well I'll be damned
if I'll do their dishes.

A Brief Affair

She hated waking up next to him
stinking of booze he'd scream
'Get me a bucket I wanna
throw up!'
He'd spent half his life
in prison.
He drank whisky constantly now.
She had to
leave him – his hide was as tough
as concrete,
she couldn't break through.
For once, Lilith misjudged – when
she left he cried his eyes out.

Lilith and the Orange Tree

The young girl stood beside me. I
Saw not what her young eyes could see:
– A light, she said, not of the sky
Lives somewhere in the Orange Tree.
SHAW NEILSON

Of course I was pulling his leg,
and didn't he lap it up – they all do,
I've pulled that trick a thousand times.

Not that some sort of light
doesn't appear, but this is always
after the fact – the poet recalling
a light was there, a light to accompany
his music of the spheres. Chills you
doesn't it? No, I don't feel bad – I never
do. In fact, I think I've brought a lot
of spiritual conviction to poetry
lovers over the years. And yes,
God does have a lot to thank me for.

Lilith Invites the Great Poet Czeslaw Milosz into Bosch's *Garden of Earthly Delights*

I

I am in the Prado watching the poet
watching the Garden of Earthly Delights.
I would like to know if he is seeking
to enter the painting or simply
to view it. Already he is calling me Eve.

I lean out and arch behind him, looking over
his shoulder at what he is writing – 'So that I run to its waters
And immerse myself in them and recognise myself.'
So far so good. But what is this talk about centuries
closing, and bodily preservation, and senses outreaching
       themselves –
his share, like mine, is nothing. He's got a nice eye for
fashion, or the lack of, I'll admit. Though he's prone
to hallucination: there is no concept of Time in this painting.

II

It was a ball because that was the shape of his shit.
Is nothing sacred?
                Or maybe it was the ball Picasso's
acrobats threw into the field of the circus.
Though for this to have been so the Prado
must have come to an agreement with the Stockholm
Gallery of Modern Art.

III

This Paradise he's writing is not true
but so beautiful I could be fooled.
He says: 'This, then, is the Fountain
Of Life? Toothed, sharp-edged,
With its innocent, delusive colour. And beneath,
Just where the birds alight, glass traps set with glue.'

He apprehends the possibility of error
built into The Scheme of Things, too human
the mystery of the fruit is the Mother
of his doom. Can Time stretch
for those trapped in the rings of his wishes?
Let me tell him, the whole lot of them,
his incredible Form included, to walk on the filth
that is my bones, my prison. Had he been Adam,
had he been Eve, he would have felt
the same satisfaction in treading on me
as he did when he uncovered the Tree's duplicity.

IV

The naming of fish, fowl, and beast,
of nakedness and conjoining, of the rich liquid
that is sap that is the blood of the sun.
Pleasure denies its connotation. I have none of this,
though maybe my outstretched fingers tickle
his groin. No matter, the stars blind the night:
'Meanwhile a flock of lunar signs fills the sky
To prepare the alchemical nuptials of the planets.'

V

There's no getting away from it, the triptych
is a death that lives in the moment that refuses
to name itself. The abyss is large and comfortable
in its actions – like the evening which gathers
beneath floodlights, like curators calling Time.

The Three Faces of Lilith

I

The three faces of Lilith
revealed themselves in glances.
Above, the air softened,
                     softened
as the three faces struggled to look
into three different hearts.

II

That behind these masks
the vegetative lurked,
                  soul vessel
shared threefold,
                  instantly recognisable,
instantly lost.

The hearts mimicked each other,
remaining unchanged, though taking
each feature as ornament.

III

Inclination and Appetite,
Frailty and Honour and Shame,
they could not flatter
and remain sane – the most obvious
attempt fell flat, strained
their solicitous natures.

IV

Virtue – picking glass
        from the upholstery
        Lilith let it be known
        she had no time
        for little red convertibles,
        lear jets, or a seat
        at the Captain's table.

Three Hearts – the First Revolution

I

The physical heart
could ward off danger
by virtue of its strength

Lilith of the physical heart
is confident, loud, enigmatic

Lilith of the physical heart
is lustful and easily
disappointed

II

The bitter heart
consumes itself,
this
is Lilith
torn by isolation,
at her most dangerous,
her most vulnerable

III

The growing heart
has an eye for itself
and will check its growth
if threatened – not that design
prevents Lilith, rather
the growing heart
knows its limits

Three Hearts – the Second Revolution

I

Lilith carries her fluid self
closer to change, keeping her back
to Gunabibi who flickers like a great snake
waiting for the sun to cloak its retreat.
The torn heart has lodged, the torn heart
has watered its blood down to the pink-orange
of cataclysm. The torn heart is dead.

II

The spiritual heart has outgrown
itself, is looking to Heaven, has cast
indiscretion aside. As the eye reaches,
climbing espaliers of sight, it crosses
the verdigris of night and spreads.

III

Full heart, blood on your copper wings,
full heart, in flight over the loveless waves,
full heart, hungering, fill yourself
with hope. Full heart, only patience
will bring Lilith back again.

Lilith's Pain

Aloof. Chest and shoulders
torn through – the three hearts
flown, flittering out like flies
from a blown carcass, though beautiful
in decay – the wings of Lilith
unfolding with her lifeblood.
And emerging from her moist cocoon,
Lilith left the trappings
of the telephone age to her old body,
and rose up out of the garden
in pursuit of the hearts.

Lilith and St Antony

She barely touches the ground,
steps so lightly, swings her tresses
or tingles with cropped hair, she dances
so sweetly, and I love her for this,
I love her because she does not tempt me ...
she is both fruitful and barren,
she inspires and empties,
her breath is dank and fresh
I love her for this ...

Lilith Considers Two Others ...

Rimbaud

To give him his due, he hated his name,
and he hated the way the scabs clustered about his
arsehole, the way governments and family
fucked him around. And he died young – in fact,
he died when he was about seven. When he noted
the colour of his mother's dresses, the texture
of his sister's undergarments, the grime
that gathered beneath his fingers. When he realised
that words were made up of letters, that letters
were devised to account for words. When he learnt
that the best poets were scatalogical; when he
made paper boats and set them loose on rivers;
when he considered the cost of clothing and arming
a soldier. When he called a name in his sleep.

Emily Dickinson

What's fifty-five years to the young at heart.
Ah, she was as supple as a six-year-old,
as sweet as a rose, as free as a butterfly.
It sounds too good to be true, doesn't it?
Well, look at it another way – she was as old
as Methuselah's mother, was old at the moment
of conception, looked me in the eye at birth
and strung together one of her weedy poems.
That she saved bits of string and wrapping paper
from Christmas, that she never got many poems
out because she begrudged paying for the postage.
So now, which version do you prefer? The one
in which her communion was with the trite,
the precious, or that with an eye to death.

Poems of Annunciation

I

the wand is as supple
as the wrist that winds
its charms

it is the strand of hair
the capillaries close to the surface,
the heart's form writ
over the page of her body

the wand is the pen
that signs off,
the signatory to arrivals
and departures

II

the message never came out
the way it was intended,
the messenger put his or her
stamp on it, soothsaying
the truth out of language
into the realm of gesture

III

Lilith sent herself
a message of hope

Lilith sent herself
a message of love

Lilith moved quickly
from the point of delivery
to the point of arrival

AND OF THE HEARTS...

Cocoons

I

Gunabibi caught the hearts
and set them to spinning
cocoons – 'I'll see you
when you get out,'
she said

II

in their transitional sleep
the hearts reconciled differences,
and the dormant merged with the actual
and meshed itself against the prospect
of a new set of rules

III

Gunabibi was surprised to see
the hearts had retained the capacity
of flight despite their long sleep
though she felt pleased with herself –
they were no longer part of Lilith,
who had long ago lost her grip on things

IV

the three faces
of one heart – steel–winged
                    iron–beaked
                                    spreading
from horizon to horizon,
                            exhaust rising
like the green dust
                    of a burst puffball.

Beyond Dürer's Nativity

The birds sit lightly, rafters slip
slowly back, stilled. Plantlife in rigid
pose abstains from growth. Enclosed
universe neat in its arch issues forth
its own angel in recognition.

An old man pours a libation of pure water.
Decay: clean and orderly. She, hands folded,
(Lilith was said to have lurked),
whispers in all tongues:
                          'il serait si doux de l'aimer...'

FULL FATHOM FIVE
(1993)

Eclogue on a Well

She stirs the waters
breaking the stone rust surface;
if the branch she holds
were longer she might
bring proof to the claim
that more than one surface
lies beneath. Even so, I defer
to her belief that the One
is solid ground – the reflection
of a deep well in a dry field.

View from a Windmill

The Chaining Tree lilts in the half-light –
thick-bodied clouds hang close to its top.
Sheep skins clot about the wooden barrels
of derelict clover-burr harvesters, dank chunks
feeding stalagmites of fat and wool formed
over fifty years of disuse. A crankshaft
rusts uncomfortably – the heart of a veteran Chev
flat-top, wheels wooden-spoked, undergoing
surgery without anaesthetic. The paddocks spread
waterlog-green, the dam eases out of its silty
fermentation – water straining through the quartz
drains, the muddy contours. And the windmill,
barely turning, its metal frame bracing the wooden
shaft, the rise and fall of seasons, forecasts
a break in the weather and drives its blades firmly
against the wind, against the winter rains.

Wheatbelt Gothic or Discovering a Wyeth

Outflanked by the sheep run, wild oats
dry and riotous, barbed wire bleeding rust
over fence posts, even quartz chunks
flaking with a lime canker, the theme
chooses itself: *ubi sunt* motif, but the verse
becomes as deceptive as an idle plough,
or a mat of hay spread over the ooze
of a dead sheep that is the floor
of the soak (blood-black beneath the skin,
bones honeycombed), crystallised with salt.

And yesteryear occluded by the viscous waters
of the stone-walled well which (on higher
ground) marks the dryness of the soak as either
delusion or lie. Only green shoots hidden
in the dead sheaths of reeds on the soak's rim
hint that water supports this travesty.

And the moon absorbs the sun, its fabric
subtlety – the undressing of a summer landscape
too blond for its own good, too much an extract:
the mid-West Gothic of a lone tree stump
that appears to beckon in its loneliness – open space
as collusive as a vaulted cathedral in Europe,
and the well as much a receptacle of guilt
as the cathedral's font. And consider the potential,
no, consider the necessity, of a flaxen-haired girl
merging in this field of vision and then erupting
from a point above the waterline, the tree stump.

Blood and Bone

Ol' Rex's son couldn't cope with the waste,
or so he said after Grace. At footy training
he claimed a morbid curiosity and a rough-'n'-
ready sense of humour. The truth be had, he
couldn't be bothered breaking his back bending
over to grab the corpses by the wool-on-their-backs
and slinging (with the correct shovelling action)
his recently collapsed livelihood onto the back
of his truck. Not even the front-end loader
which his neighbour – the footy coach – favoured:
trench graves and barrows to remind the forgetful,
   stimulate the thin-skinned folk visiting
   from the city. No, he favoured the tractor
   and disc ploughs set in tandem: the drought
recently broken and the ground needing preparation
(anyway). No, he just ploughed them in. Instant
   blood and bone. Organic fertiliser as underlay
for the carpet of spray he applied just in case
   modern weeds couldn't (or wouldn't) understand
the older methods of control. Furthermore, it should
be said, ol' Rex's son realised that there were ironies
contained in his actions that he couldn't (or shouldn't)
even begin to realise. And if ol' Rex knew of them
he kept it quiet, refusing to discuss the incident
                at any price.

Ersatz

Clouds outwit the light meter
as the shutter lifts

Salt, like ground ice, scaffolds
stray blades of grass;
the water table rises

and brings to air an aspro bottle,
its mud-encased body shattered.

Not made larger though brought closer
the paddocks to the east no longer rise
but slide into the immediate ground:
a theory evolves – it's all based
on triangles and collusion, the patterning
of landform and occupation
linked to longer walks
and evenings spent on the
                              verandah.

                              The graveyard
(are there rules here concerning area?) lies
amongst sheep-death carnage, at a point
of concentrated takings: earlier
a fog tamped down the rough edges,
welded dust and clouds
into a smooth if rippled seam.

Carcass of Sheep in Fork of Dead Tree

A set up. The carcass slung
over a fork in a dead tree,
the line-of-sight unbroken
from shearing shed, perfect
for high-powered rifles
with telescopic lenses
hungry for *predators*. You see,
certain birds think nothing
of rotting sheep climbing
dead trees. Nor, at a later
date, when the ribcage
has become the staves
of an ark stranded by flood,
of a photographer convincing
his subject to sit naked

beneath the wreckage, the grey
branches – side stretched
such that the nipple closest
to the camera becomes
as sharp as the eye
    a bullet.

Guiding James Dickey Around Wheatlands

Long rifle high velocity bullets
shed hot spots on settling,
their flowered heads spent in clay
or buried in flesh. The shadows

of firing actually light up the night
like flintlocks, muzzle-loaders,
though there is peace now, and you,
James Dickey, creep behind the contour

banks and dam walls, rainwater tanks
and machinery, your arrows dancing
in their quiver, bow aching to be
strung and stretched, as if atmosphere

is target enough, as if the movement
of shaft to string is all that matters.
And the air here is clear – whispering
in the short bristles of cold light,

coiling about the wound's opening,
dropping its hood of dried blood.
Let it be said, there is peace here and now:
the lull after the storm, the prayers

of thanksgiving. The brass cases of rimfire
bullets are to be sold as scrimshaw, and while
Queequeg shall fill our beds with shrunken death
we'll accept even this as quaint and curious.

Strobe: The Road from Toodyay to New Norcia

Separated by red vinyl interior,
inertia belts like strips of asphalt,
the road absorbing and yet occluding,
dark sunglasses cannot prevent light
destroying direction, severing
the bas-relief of thought and the nausea
of being shredded by a sun strobed
through branches spread like braids
of dank, clotted hair over the decolletage
of the road. Strafed by lightfall,
eyes disseminate across the windscreen,
the dashboard is sharp and the lowered
shades bludgeon the optic nerve.
The interior sun is a calmative red.

The Song of Buoyancy

The river rips the body
and charges a spiralling path:
a ceilidh where the singers
and the speakers are rapid
voiced and flowing towards
the markers; the sky, anodised.

That suspended, the body
divines another life, the mind
willing to second its right
of navigation to the tide
and current and waves
that massage the waterline.

Prospectus

A sailboard cuts the path of a ketch
in full flight, the river a black thermal.
The child concentrates on the sailboard,
its luminous sail and sharp movement.
The father watches the crew of the ketch
heaving to, waving their hands furiously.
Judge and jury, the outcome of their
separate trials is different – decisions
hang over the jetty, land-bound, looking
riverward, aching for the isolation
of open waters, the wind's strong hands
gripping the mast, flexing the sail,
a threat beyond the scope of a glass.
The middling swell chops at the pylons,
a slap across the face for quarrelling
couples, the minutes sliced from their
lives. Somewhere, the father's lover,
the child's mother, rides oceanwards
against the weather, unaware of the impending,
the possible, the likely, thinking only
of yachts, the water, her first sailing.

On Looking into the Canning River from Deep Water Point Jetty and Seeing Paul Klee Staring Back

The leaf of a blue lupin floats sharply
past, a bayonet in livery, and cuts
a stern visage looking up at me.
Like a courtier's poems circulated
amongst the ranks of the tactlessly
discreet, or paper boats with ensigns.

My face blank as a witness kept in a safe-house,
amnesty like vanishing crème de menthe.
That I have here, with others, smoked the collected works
of Wallace Stevens, my soul as drawn as my lungs, as
drawn as the eyes of a gull inciting food,
as drawn as rivers like our own seeking the sea.
That I have launched myself from this jetty
and sought a buoy singing crazy in the vacillation
of a jet boat's planing, the skier in its wake
swinging to cut me off, shaving the brief horizon.
That I have reduced to three shapes the Phantom
logic of flow – the shape of the river, the jetty, sky's curve.
That I have, with others, lamented knowing
of those who turned out murderers whose crimes
are unwritable, who used this river as a dumping
ground for the booty they'd stripped from their victims' bodies.
That I have, with others, run scared from steel-strapped
boxes laden with drugs and protected by large calibred
American pistols and longed for its riddling waters.
That I have carved the letters of futility into my lower
leg, a rough draft I carry always
that dragged in these waters turns a background black
and smoulders with the look of a fading sun.
That the headless lady who has apparently
returned to sideshow alley was once and probably still is
the sister of Gary Brophy
who at the age of twelve
rode his motorbike inside the Globe of Death and sat with me
on the end of Deep Water Point jetty
observing the tribulations of punctured blowfish,
whose mother was Zelda the snake-woman,
whose father was a tout at the boxing tent.
That a friend drowned himself in your image
searching for the way, escaping the stern visage.

Fritz Lang of the Streams

The killer cables the news
and the world polarises
black and white.
The fish are blocked
from moving upstream.
Spanish mackerel, the formula
ones of the coast, are intercepted
from the air. Over a glass of water
and a banana I joke – our eyes
lapse into pools of mist
and rise shakily towards
the dawn of a new age.
Baitfish swim in the rockpools
and Fritz Lang of The Streams
moves closer to the ocean
where images compile themselves
like tides. Later, a video
recaptures the takings.
In desperation the viewers
compile a poem. It includes
the word death no less than six times.
Of friends, relatives, poets.
Fish-death is mentioned once –
the lesser half of a simile.
Fritz Lang doesn't rate a mention,
unless it be that the rocky coastline
is described as a decaying city:
dark, sentient, impelling.

Endgame

Who upon chewing glass
to a point where his lips, cheeks, and tongue
became a viscous paste

then took his leave
calling on the regenerative powers
of the river
and found a jetty from which to launch
his healing swim
who finished his can of emu bitter
and placed his shoes and the bulk of his clothes
neatly by the iron-knuckled
capstans

Black Rain Folio: Three Poems in Memory of Craig Elson Loney

1 *'Black Rain is Falling on the Himalayas –
the centre of a constantly moving universe.'*

Black rain is falling on the Himalayas – the centre
        of a constantly moving universe.
Vast leaden clouds plume-down heavy rain, rivers run
slowly over the face of Annapurna; in the coffee shops
        tourists joke it's the colour of Nepalese hash.
Black rain is falling on the Himalayas – the trekkers
and Sherpas have confirmed. The centre made liquid
        and night-bound, the cancered lung
wrung dry, acrid, pernicious, not the centre but the outer
        wall of a smoke ring stagnating.

2 *The Mark of the Beast*

The mark of the beast is a cairn of granite
        or the rain-riven walls of a dam
shining in the late afternoon like a vast lump
        of crumpled velvet and polished bone.
The mark of the beast is an old foundry surrounded
    by rubble and lime pits, the navigation marker
that lures or deters to save, the glint of distant
        sunglasses.

The mark of the beast sits comfortably
beneath the frayed wool and clotted skin of sheep bloated
    with wheat plundered from a broken silo.

3 *In-folio*

Television cameras film the police photographers
            positioning the body. Still life.
A stapler on the corner of a desk. A point of reference.
A service revolver hangs glibly. The eye of the camera
        is moon silver. Outside, the river inflects
and Jean Genet's *Querelle of Brest* looks deep into
a burnt orange sun that refuses to set. Tourists come
            and photograph the simple buildings
that make up a policeman's ashram. They have read the laws,
    have seen the brochures. Some prostrate themselves.

Roundhouse

*Built in 1830/31 on the headland on the south side of the Swan River
mouth, the Roundhouse was Western Australia's first gaol.*

Windscale on a pitted cenotaph collects
In the seascroll, the script, the brocade
Of a foaming, spreading hand – shoalwaters

Where the polished caprock tightens the little
Space – though the sky expands amongst
The mental rigging, adhering itself to a calenture –

Deep green, the sooty terns rock on the lip
And then flip back into oblivion. Windscale
In its sharp climb should incite an angrier sea:

The barebone, the spit's jawjut, the anchorage
Of rock and shore, aspirations for games
On the sky's field of play – cenotaph – mutiny...

218

The Phenomena that Surround a Sighting of Eclipse Island

1   *The Gap: A Paradox*

I speak to you elementally
and at a distance
that becomes
the depth
of an ocean
that in being southern
and arctic
in impression
absorbs all blues
and is the deeper for this.

Darkness wells
from the fathoms
of the palette
as I paint
an expression –
my footholds
prone to slippage:
hard rock stacked
like soft lozenges
sucked by cyclopean
giants who'd smashed
aside savage breakers
to sear bone-black cliffs –
like The Gap
through which I peer; place
of the freak wave,
back-stabbing gale,
and brutal rain.

Place where
a neighbour
of my brother's
threw herself
mandraxed and furious
into this suicide

machine only
to survive
and find herself
a landlubber
farming children
with the names
of sea-nymphs. Place
where keening landfall
sea-meets and rifles
moods, like a gale
springing the bleak staves
of a broken container ship.
Place where phenomena
shape themselves like
the vertebrae of whales
tormented by water,
wind, and sun –
anchored to the coastline
by harpoons requisitioned
from the magazines
of scuttled whale-chasers
limping sulkily
icewards.

2   *The Blowholes – A Lust Recalled*

Not firing today.
Unless I've plunged
over the cliffs and into
the Prussian blue waters
without their noticing –
drawn by the spell
of Eclipse Island.
Somewhere she holds
her heart in her mouth,
clenched firmly
between pearled teeth,
his tongue flickering
about the blockage
like an astringent.

3 *Stray Pockets of Diffident Weather*

The way rocks
just below the surface
incite the ocean,
frustrate it into action:
the flurry of white-water
luminescent greens
and the slick white
of glossy house-paint.

Consider again your foothold –
Eclipse Island spiriting
the sheets of solidified flesh,
the stray pockets
of diffident weather
moving between fronts.

4 *Eclipse Island?*

Well, I was just waiting
and then I got to thinking
about lighthouses – I could see
two of them from my *vantage point* – one
on the mainland, another on Eclipse Island;
and I thought of the candy-striped
lighthouse I'd shown you in Geraldton
and of that lighthouse just down
from your sister's place looking like
a white bishop from our chess set.
And I realised how easy it would be
for others to misconstrue my missing you
(as). Anyway, it's just not true.

5 *The Ship's Log: The Colophon*

Sheer
waste
this spray
moving skywards
like

an inverted
parachute.
The sun drinks
in the layers
holding
heavy weather
close
to the water.
We shape
an itinerary
of arrivals
and departures.
A footnote
is added
like bad breath
to a deep kiss
in an impressionable
place –
later in life
they dressed well
and cared
generally
about
their
appearance.
The ship's log full
I make
for shore.

6 *The Camera*

Why do you give me
so many opportunities to make a fool
of you anyway? You ask?
Like the tourist
caught on the lip of The Gap
unable to edge his way back,
the camera about his neck
tapping at the rocks
like a sick pendulum,
his head weighing
more than it should.

222

Breath, an icy pocket,
opens ultramarine,
a dry sea
tracking its glacial
course   beyond
Eclipse Island
and beyond
the course,
cancelling
as the tides
rip back and forth
covering all earth,
a mosaic impressed
upon the potential
arrangements
of itself.
Lapis lazuli,
a gift ultramarine,
blended in the swirl
of the sun indeterminate
above the clouds –
the locals saying
it's just an ordinary
summer's day,
which is their way
and our solution.

Unseasonal Weather on the Outskirts

I

at the base
desiccated foliage
washes itself
in a font of dust

the canopy lowered,
the clouds scribble
their epistle
in shadows over
the bones of hill

the warmth wells up
from the centre,
disbands in dried tops,
splits tree skins
with a lugubrious sigh

II

navigating the scrub's
tidal leanings
bearded dragons
mark sandcharts
with swathing tails

bronzewings fossick
amongst the tailings
of dry sclerophyll forest,
their thoughts writ
in water

Swarm

Black fire with an orange heart
rages amongst the red branches
of the swarm-tree. I tell her it's
temporary, like last year.
The hive, high in a hollow
in the neighbours' yard, erupts
and sparks. Our son bursts
through the flywire door
screaming *bees!* as if their

frantic clamour were drums of war.
It hangs bristling and fluid,
its mystery an optical illusion.
A midday astronomy – the eye
of the telescope scorched
and holding the cold heat
of space. Towards evening
the swarm lifts and rolls
chaotically downwind,
settling its orange cowl
about the dark outline
of a tree.

Exposing the *Rhizanthella gardneri* Orchid

Above the roots
of a Broom Honey Myrtle
the beak of an orchid
tastes the acrid air.
Its mouth sweet with flowers.
Termites roaming the pollen.

Saprophyte,
and guest-host
to a root-invading fungus,
its liaisons go unnoticed
as the scrub is peeled back,
and are only half-revealed
with the lifting
of the surface.

Excavated,
its leaves unfold
and termites roam the pollen,
its dark heart
reddening
with exposure.

Hills / Storm Rabbit

Sunset erupts and collapses
into a feeding city – wavering
                           buckling
the luminous cloud blossoming
in its own light, polyp on polyp,
the collecting rubble and heavy airs,
sand and charred stumps, retaining
the thin line of sea that could expand
either way, washing speculation aside,
frothing at the base of standpoint.
It is the storm that centres,
the immediacy of the electric claw
– etcher of the finite Grace –
the light without fed through
pinpricks in a cardboard sky.

From our coastal vantage point
we watch as the tale of the rabbit
unfolds – withdrawn via third forces,
seconded to hill, inheriting storm,
pupils reddening, carmine calyx
unfurling ...

Transpositions

Suppressing the sheer – au naturel –
a black granite rockface is replaced
by a video screen as large as the telecom
building.
                    How's this for a trick? We strike
the screen and a black stream gushes   forth /

it's these polyester-rayon threads we're
wearing, they give the impression
of being wet
when in fact they're as dry as a black granite
rockface on a mid-summer's day.
                              Walkway 2
might lead us to the controls: contrast, brightness,
colour, though who needs them? The sky
looks better orange, and the dull grey water
might even be clean enough to drink.

The Dam Busters

(for John Forbes)

A brown-shouldered kite's plunge
mimics the deep hum of a high voltage
powerline in damp weather, its angular
flight pinpointing departure
on the dam's curved wall. The science
we have learnt to mistrust
lurks smugly behind steel-plated doors,
our safety resting surreally
in its neo-classical charms,
while a bomber with a swollen stomach
approaches at low altitude
and you mutter under your breath
'everyone that fucks up gets shot down'.

Letter to Anthony Lawrence

Blinkered, the sun's eye stretches
but still can't see 'round corners;
and this is *no* heresy. The rhythm
builds on the faintest repetition:
a flower's whisper screaming cyclones
out of innocence. So, what's new?
The Settlement's fluid stone continues
to lead astray, too often pissing
on bins and taking umbrage when told
it's not in place. The plan is to
quietly slip a synchromesh gearbox
into its midst during the year's
last footy match. The Americans have
done it time and again with the Superbowl
leaving one sort of death in the streets,
another in the living room. This, my friend,
burns deeper scars than those of lighthouses
buried under skin, of mulesing shears
the arse of a fretting lamb.

The Confederates are weeping
on Monument Hill, the League
is scratching its wounds
in the Cultural Centre, still
Henry Moore roams the public spaces,
a transvestite with hollowed guts.
The Caller sprays birdshit
from its mouth – too much calling
too far North. The Gascoyne will
overflow and stain paper like blood.
The call of a European raven garottes
the suburbs in their Spring strife!
Confidence flexed in lurex, tans
bubbling beneath umbrellas. A speedboat
sheers the lampposts, marking
with a steady, rivery dribble
the hidden lines of the road.

There is a resident widow-maker
centering the back garden. Its name
is Sinisgalli and it speaks Italian.
    'Si può prendere la felicità
    per la coda come un passero.
    Si possono dimenticare i debiti
    che abbiamo con il mondo.'
it seems to be saying over and over.
Sometimes I sit at its base
praying for an answer, in translation.

The hills are alive with the sound
of jackhammers. The air is salt and silt.
The flame-leaf tones over, for the better.
And wisteria hangs rudely over
my window, cutting out sound,
ingesting light. I am thinking
of Proclamation Tree, of Yagan,
of shadows stretching more lives
than either of us would care to remember.

Corpses

1

Slung out over the barrel
like a sack of wet hessian

its claws and ivory chip teeth
beginning to yellow

its fur drying in thick
poisonous quills

its skull emblazoned
with pearls of rapidly

tarnishing ratshot.

2

Tail beginning to hollow,
parchment skin sized

in its own tallow,
dumped contorted

amongst balding Michelins,
a boomer locked between

roo bar and asphalt.

3

Barely golden, its fleece
glints lustrously

when the sun mounts
the tree its grave.

Slung in the three-branched fork
its anatomy hovers.

The skull, expressionless,
glares awkwardly

back over its shoulder.

A Note on the Butcher

Removing his apron,
ambiguously striped
Prussian blue and zinc white,
the butcher opens the door
of a sky-blue car, interior
withered vermilion,
to be greeted by a tiger,
neck on a thread,
bobbing its striped head,
eyes lolling savagely.

Of

Of emulsifiers and preservatives
extracted from boiled-down animal,
of houses with walls of horse hair
and thongs of leather to restrain
the tortured awning,
of feet covered in dead cow,
kangaroo, crocodile ...
the business of pig-skin briefcases,
of those whose guilt lies in fish,
of those sucking the nectars
of sacred beasts,
of the differences between *clean* and *dirty* flesh,
of those who seek truth in the burnt offering,
of 'perfect and upright' Job, slaughterer
who sought to appease over and over,
of *Julius Civilus with a Dead Cock*
arrogantly accepting what *is*
over and over, back and forth, to and fro.

Window Shopping at the Taxidermist's

The permeable glass – sieve-like – drains
the liquid light, a fluid more precious
than formaldehyde, the smell of life ...
A grimace or a grin stretches like a trap,
and as a backdrop a deer dispenses
with its claim to needing a heart,
it's only there from the neck up,
though its eyes are sharp, senses finely
tuned, nervousness held in check
through a familiarity born of sharing
a display case with a pack of wolves.
The window shoppers hunt amongst the grime
of the city's unglamorous side, their prey
the glimmering skin, the combed and shining –
here they show their skill, knowing
where to bag the finest trophy.

Incense

A fumigation of the emotions, heady
diatribe – olfactory pleasure offset
by eyelids red, swollen, and weeping:
a Cubist interpretation made fluid.
Patchouli – The Enforcer – desire
pushed to the cone's red centre,
an appeasing of the angry God.
Sandalwood – The Sleeper – latent
thoughts brought forth, lulled
into conversation, the Truth Drug.
Jasmine – The Subtle – works its way
into the picture after the smoking's
done, a faint scent lingers like an air

of suspicion. And finally, frankincense –
The Stakhanovite – straight to the point,
muscle-bound worker transferring sense
from source to target, the sweetness
coming with a job well done. Incense,
habeas corpus allowing none to escape
its call – the body its witness, the heart
its victim, its end *a sus. per coll*
for Heat, Lust, and a sweet-scented Haze
existing unto itself: *carpe diem.*

ludruk

clown and transvestite

there are no criminals in this street
just new cars

there are no criminals in this street
just new cars

so new they outshine their owners
who couldn't be called dull

not dull, considering their jewellery
which is really an accessory like the car

like the car they are very new and shiny
and there are no criminals in this street

very new and shiny unlike their eyes
which are so hungry

they wouldn't think car or jewellery,
there are no criminals in this street

Batak House and Mushroom Girl

She is looking for a way out,
and her Batak house seems
the only hope. She lures
Westerners with the promise
of animist dreams, of a kaleidoscope
of ancestral loves and fears.
Sleep tonight in my Batak house,
you are beautiful and I am beautiful too ...
sleep in my Batak house and you shall
be safe from the spirits wandering
the fields, rising from the depths
of the lake ...

Editing

The cutback comes not by way
of a flick-knife – that's 'switch-blade'
breaking out cross-hatch with a flash
if you're from the wrong side of the track –
and pays no regard to whether or not
you're wearing the latest Reebok Pumps,
or a Thai-American hand-woven baseball cap.
Intervals appear only when the audience
is spread thinly about the rail carriage,
clutching their sportswear. Spread as thinly
as the moon waning like a prop with a broken
collarbone, as thinly as a metaphor that to keep
track has had to change tune and colour
and renounce additions to the body altogether.

Disclaimers

1st Disclaimer

The mescal-eyed doctor gloats and worries simultaneously.
    Hedging his bets, enjoying the demystification
Of insanity, the keeping track of a heartbeat, body's
Electricity. There've been no horrific injuries this shift
    To unsettle his matter-of-fact, *That's life*
    attitude. Just the basket case scraping
The floor, complaining about a telegram from India that
Provided nothing but lines running off the paper's edge.

2nd Disclaimer

You can play any number of identities but they've all got
    The same voice and behave in exactly the same way.
They like the same food, drink, entertainment. They love
Exactly as the others would, have the same hates and fears.
    Thus far escape from any one of them has proved
    Impossible. For one to exist the others remain.
We are necessary they say. We are positive and good in our
    Intentions. We deserve full recognition.

3rd Disclaimer

Sempiternal, the poet speaks for his own language, in the
    Gutter he is great. Amongst tears reasonless
And caught not in the city but the concept of city, he
Plants ambiguity without self-criticism. The tears and
    Actuality of being there are enough reason for this.
    The circuit-breakers favour self pity and a city
Is the best place for this. It adds intensity. There is no
    Room for dilution, no open space.

4th Disclaimer

From the gaming table to the early opener, the risk of needle
      Stick not obvious with the first mescal, though sex-traps
Skirt the dance floor and eye its centre, a lavender swirl
Opaque with dry ice, a paradox of people cloistered in the wild,
      The State of Nature Realigning, the recognition
      In a drama of substances, the solitary actor holding
The cup high, projecting his voice at the light-etched ceiling,
Calling for more, the recognition inadequate – a ploy, a foil.

Testaments Renewed

> *So let him take to beggary*
> *Since fate thereto doth him constrain.*

> from 'The Testament' by FRANÇOIS VILLON

I

My country does not own me, so let it
advance beyond hearsay, did he or she
      ever notice that their child
      had big ears and a shining nose?
As a three-year-old he built skyscrapers.

And O that Spleen, that early morning Spleen:
as poisonous as a dugite's kiss, as deadly
      as the juice rung from a butt
      and supped outside nightclubs, hungry
for a piece of the action ... spitting at bouncers.

The Ballade of Hypocrisies

No wool – no, we do not sleep on wool –
even between cotton sheets *vanitatum vanitas*:

Youth and its pleasures are but snares
and now the punishment amply repays the justice,

236

a bed of nails, dank stone, and bars on the doors
can do no more than put pleasure in a vice.

II

When he shared the madman's view that food
and drink were like the books in a second-hand
      shop with a barber in the backroom
      telling his customers of watered-down
whiskey, he decided he'd grown up enough to leave.

Of book bindings and 55 tests to check the type
of sizing used on the paper – the first chemistry
      since the prospects of a great career
      in research – he sought to appease
his curiosity. Older and organic he rings the factory.

Last heard the Queen Mother was choking on a fishbone.
Cops look through the front window of a fishmonger's
      shop and count the hours they've got left
      before knock-off. It's late-night shopping.
Necessity drives distraught patrons towards the law.

Ballade to This Country

Despite holding my body in the cradle of its love
this country does not hold right of tenure over me.

Despite Social Securities and my debt therein
this country does not hold right of tenure over me.

I make my own pain and don't need any extra,
thank you all the same. This country does not own me.

I shall not even hope to attain the lifespan of a fly
despite this country telling me it grants longer lives.

This land is not even this country's to give away,
this country does not hold right of tenure over me.

Monuments and the Nemesis of Love: almost a prayer

Blok's Copernican monument on
    top of the sphere

The poor placing the Just on
    top for good luck

The right of intervention becomes
    the nemesis of love

III

Of sacred decrees, let them all know,
they just want to fuck you with their
    lubricated dreams – this is the city
    that gets off on bankcards and creams,
that offers hope with each bottle of beer.

What is unfolding here should be obvious by now:
Cerberus, Orpheus, and the Lord Mayor, have
    got together to create a scene,
    swell the city's coffers with spy
machines. How else could they possibly know

    That when Sir Walter Raleigh received his final call
he said, *And when I took the Fall, And when I rescinded*
    and yet remained obligatory to your
    borrowed pain ... And how else could they know
that he heard the call and caught a train to Armadale.

'The lonely of heart is withered away': reduced

1

The cricket pitch is a glowing strip,
calenture betrayed by reticulation.
Carpet over concrete. Fluorescent green.
The ball should bounce with regularity
though tears and nicks give some hope
to the bowler on what should be
a batsman's paradise.

The matrix of the streets read in the fragments
of head-drawn mud. A gannet on a truck tyre,
purple swamphens stalking the outer limits
of bulrushes that know no inland.
Already the Council is filling it in.
The swamp, they say, is rising,
the suburb sinking.

The fine print hints that I'm avoiding the issue
or even incapable of exploding the truth.
OK, then I'll say it, but with another's voice:
'The lonely heart's withered away.' Satisfied?
We walk crisply, out of the picture.

2

I've been trying to remove all trace of moisture
from my thought and body. Depriving one does not
unfortunately
mean depriving the other. To remove all trace
of moisture
both the mind and the body
need to be ambidextrous.
Head-banging to the Ramones in a hothouse on a forty
degree day, staying awake for three days on ice from Hawaii,
pulling the plunger out of a pick stilled in your vein,
donating your tear ducts.
Laughter helps.

3

Hyper-realism: the glass blower collates
flecks of his inner world and forgets
they're part of him. A yacht in a snow storm,
the lunar meltdown as love blackens
the walls of his mouth. His body a cylinder
overfilled
with gas.
His breath as dry as a blowtorch.

4

She has a part in this.
So damned considerate he is she thinks.
He'll even chop
the rhythm about
to free her. So damned considerate he is she thinks.

5

Maitre d'hotel plies them with drinks.
Maitre d'hotel sees to their needs and lisps
to the bellboy, gives a sly wink to his wife
not far enough away but cosy on the telephone.
Look
he says
look, I bet you can see it from there,
the heart is lonely,
the heart is withered away.
Funny, the drinks haven't even wet their lips.

Sexual Politics in Eadweard Muybridge's
Man Walking, After Traumatism of the Head

1

He could easily be
A man walking, after traumatism
Of the head.
There's something vaguely Platonic about this.
Francis Bacon, lip-synching
His way through smugness, injecting passion and/or lust
Into Muybridge's studies of wrestlers: 'Actually,
Michelangelo and Muybridge
Are mixed up in my
Mind together, and so I perhaps
Could learn about positions
From Muybridge
And learn about the ampleness,
The grandeur of form
From Michelangelo...' This is not tongue-in-cheek,
And why should it be she cries?
At the end of the day
Folly counts for nothing, she says
Majestically, the banana light glowing
Sedately by the bedhead, Foucault
Powerless and fading.

2

What moral autonomy remains
As, from frame to frame,
He walks. Why aren't you a panel beater?
She asks as your last thought spills
To the floor and scatters.

Muybridge considered
Leland Stanford's Quest To Prove
All Four Legs Of A Trotting Horse
Are Off The Ground Simultaneously
At A Particular Moment ... earlier
He'd been a fly on the wall
As Muybridge blew his wife's

Dashing, cavalier lover away...
'omne animal triste post coitum'.

Sadness comes quickly
And he wonders about
The contents of his blood.
And panel beaters would find
The passive role
Difficult
To shape.

3

Sharing a cell with lust
In the prison of desire
He remarked that the form
Of his cell-mate was a little peculiar:
Casanova moving with the gait
Of one who has succumbed
To animal locomotion, an electro-photographic
Investigation of consecutive phases
Of animal movement.

She says that he measures progress
With his penis, a well-oiled dip stick:
Her body absorbing the entire jungle
Of his body which is ecologically sound,
Creeping out of its rich enclave
And seeking to make the barren lush.
He believes that you can't get off
On rape, that violence is mental
Sickness.
I like his manners – c'est tout –
She confesses.

4

A skull fractured
Does not necessarily
Mean liberation
On the afterdeath plane
Nor freedom for the oppressed mind.
LSD, a freak in drag,
Denies the mind is lodged
In the skull, that it is
Part of the body. The dozens or so
Blotters found in his pocket
Have nothing to do
With his portfolio
Of deviance.
He's on top of it,
And knows the yellow haze
Suppressing the landscape
Is merely ash
In the upper-atmosphere.
The signature is this: it hurts
To cum on bad acid, but did that
Ever deter you?

5

His head is traumatised
By dehydration, his brain shrinking.
Starvation has frayed the linkages
Between spinal cortex and legs.
His walk is one of decline
Interrupted by hope.
He feels spent and thin.
Men eat to vomit and vomit to eat.
Seneca tells us; and no woman can be too rich or too thin.
Chastity is starvation
Starvation is traumatism of the head.

6

She hates the hype
But loves the splendour:
The page written she relinquishes
Her rights to the material
Inherently hers. The moral community
Is concerned only with growth
At the end of the day – he tells them
That he is hers and couldn't give a shit.
Does she reciprocate they say?
Would you – a man walking,
With a traumatism of the head?

7

Underwire bras and jockstraps
Entangle a chicken desperately
Lunging, a torpedo already
Within range of its tail feathers,
Rudely muzzling its way
Through a sea of discharge.
So, this is love? it asks.
Muybridge screams from his observation post
'Keep the bloody thing within the gridwork!
Calibrate, calibrate! for God's sake
It's all comparative.' Stripping off
He rushes the chicken and wrestles it,
'Damn the torpedoes, keep the cameras rolling!'
Duchamp's Nude descends a staircase
While Meissoner, de Neuville, Detaille,
Remington, Malevich, and Giacomo Balla,
Watch on excitedly.

8

When size doesn't matter
You'd better start asking questions.
I mean, it's all or nothing
Isn't it. As for what's behind it ...
A magnet *does* have *two* poles.
Self control, the object of pleasure:

Every orgasm a spot in time
Without the lacework.
And this all about walking,
With a traumatism of the head,
The lexicon spread as three rednecks
Smash you over the skull with iron-knuckled
Fists, or an overdose of speed threatens
To burst capillaries, or glass lodged in a crescent
Below your left eye dislodges and unplugs
The contents of your identity.
The time lapse between frames shortens
And your collapse is traced
More minutely. Hasten slowly.

9

Porn is the Theory.
Rape is the Practice.
A sign held by a youth
In Minneapolis.
A skirt stained with sweat
Radiates in a bath
Of yellow dye.
The gate is locked,
The fences high.
She, sunbaking,
Looks over her shoulder,
Her tan slipping away:
In a tree perches
Her neighbour,
A glint in his eye.

10

Stripping thought
He dreamt an anthology,
Visual and responsive.
Reflections on the obvious.
A spring day and I'm full of hate.
Stuff like that.
He would include
A photograph by Muybridge,

(Who after disposing of Major Larkyns
Apologised to the ladies
And settled to a newspaper).
Though not one of his locomotion
Sequences, whose implication
Goes beyond a book, but of the Colorado
In dry dock accompanied by an anonymous
Muybridge on Contemplation Rock
Later used as proof of madness.
And on the title page a quote
From the *San Francisco Daily
Evening Post*: 'Little
Did Muybridge dream
As he bent over
The bedside of his wife
And he caressed her,
That Larkyn's kisses
Were yet fresh and hot
Upon her lips.'

Max Dupain's *Floater* Weighs Anchor and Makes for the Trade Routes

Good thing Dupain appreciated depth-of-field,
This floater was targeted to one side
of the frame the same way
an incidental branch or vine
might dress a travel snap. Too bad
it developed a mind of its own and defied
the layout, weighing anchor
and making for the trade routes.
A slow tide playing havoc
with the hull of the body
and the sun warping the decks.
The figurehead expressionless.

Interpreting the Swan River Through the Eyes
of Frances Possessed by Arthur Boyd's
Bathers At Shoalhaven

It's seasonal – you'd write a different poem in winter.
It's topographical – it depends where you're locating the image.
It's situational – hot weather and a public holiday
    being the ingredients for disaster.

The flensed corpses – sun articulated bodies, their diets
written in flesh, or lack of, with tissue at the mercy of hormones,
the artist's sense of perspective. A speedboat carves a watery
    slice and dresses their bodies briefly.

Floundering – marooned – abandoned – flotsam and jetsam,
the dirty rim of the river's basin. Targets of soft-serve icecream
vans, vendors of blood and bone, cigarette companies. Clouds swelter.
    Their hearts are waterlogged, swimming the vast unknown.

Well hung, low slung – lugubrious breasts, buttocks,
stomachs, and testicles. And these are the beautiful ones.
It's enough to give you a complex she says. At Shoalhaven
    swimmers have grown flippers, the dogs are muzzled.

Full Fathom Five

On viewing a reproduction of Full Fathom Five
in Ellen G. Landau's Jackson Pollock, *and thinking
over the recent death of a friend by drowning.*

> *Full fathom five thy father lies;*
>   *Of his bones are coral made;*
> *Those are pearls that were his eyes.*
>   *Nothing of him that doth fade*
> *But doth suffer a sea change*
>   *Into something rich and strange.*
>
>   SHAKESPEARE
>   *The Tempest,* 1.II

> *Five fathoms out there. Full fathom five thy father lies. At once
> he said. Found drowned. High water at Dublin bar. Driving before
> it a loose drift of rubble, fanshoals of fishes, silly shells. A corpse
> rising saltwhite from the undertow, bobbing landward, a pace a pace
> a porpoise. There he is. Hook it quick. Sunk though he be beneath
> the watery floor. We have him. Easy now.*
>
>   JAMES JOYCE,
>   *Ulysses*

1

Gallery-wise it rates
as a painting
of unfathomable depth.
On my desk it is the surface
of a puddle or an ocean.
As they say, you can drown
in both.

2

I've a great uncle who captained
a bullion ship
which capsized during a storm
rounding the Horn. These
the 'eroded treasures'
noted by Landau
as occurring in the swells
and rips of paint?

3

There he is. Hook it quick.

Full fathom five
dredged deep
the glory
of drowning
in a river
or taking to sea
and being dragged
back to shore.
The hook as sharp
as sight honed
by shamans,
the corpse a prismatic
reflection
of the living body.

Chaotic fish
dissect currents,
dislocate reefs,
and scatter sandbanks.
They will not be recruited
as pallbearers.

4

Full? What if the ocean's floor
is fluxive? A mixture
of excrement and bone,
lime-slurry and sand,
mud and decaying tissue?
Full fathom five
multiplied. The formula
variable. A multi-storied
apartment or funeral
parlour? If so
the basement
is never featured
in the catalogues
or brochures.

5

Full fathom five
the eyes burn
the undertow,
state-changing: vaporous,
liquid, solid.
A body's flow-down
arrests pollution, death
a notion of the surface.
I submerge the image.

6

Pebbles and tacks
pennies and buttons
a pair of keys
combs and matches
cigarettes and paint
tube tops
fallen overboard
and swallowed
by dense sweeps
of effluent
and colouring
agents.

7

In finding his way
Pollock may have joined
the path of suicides,
the ocean a forest
through which you
approach the circles
of Inferno (molten,
drenched in spirits).
The jewels of distortion
shine in the blue-green
flurries, and the wreckage
of a brief life unwinds
the silver threads
of darkness.

The Healing of the Circle

(a response to Jackson Pollock's painting
The Moon Woman Cuts the Circle, *c. 1943)*

If Jung or Miró or Picasso had a hand in this
the moon woman is not saying. If her name
should be Nokomos, daughter of the bright
moon and grandmother of Hiawatha, then she
spilt from the moon when her swing failed
to cut through a suitor's jealousy.
Critics list Picasso's *Girl Before*
a Mirror, Miró's *Person Throwing a Stone*
at a Bird, and the obligatory Jungian symbology,
in this case appearing as a Haidi tattoo –
'The woman in the moon'. Regardless, the moon
woman stares straight through them. The blue
background is blood starved of oxygen, blood
extracted before conception of moon woman
and offspring. The red is too brilliant,
only the gullible fire with blood-thirst
and the iconography of sacrifice. The ritual
is desertion that patterns a necessary
distraction; the head-dress an identity.

Lavender Mist

(after Jackson Pollock)

An overcast day, drizzle drifts in over the coast,
jacketing factories, like propylene sheets
between buildings. lavender mist
sickly sweet, read in a trance
the fault threatens to burst, the shell crater
unravelling its fused heart, what forces
moving over the border? lavender mist
is the moment before death, shrapnel
silently cutting its way through lace curtains
while you look down onto the sea, lavender
mist, pot-pourri, you watch it swallow
the wharves, the first waves of the cold war.

251

Vonal-Ksz

Painting and sculpture become anachronistic terms: it is more exact to speak of bi-, tri-, and multi-dimensional plastic art. We no longer have distinct manifestations of a creative sensibility, but the development of a single plastic sensibility in different spaces.
VICTOR VASARELY

I   *fields of blue*

fields of blue
variable
slip under borders
though in doing so
alter/fed
through different spaces
a field of blue
spreads itself
maybe
through the impossible/
the reading of the monochromatic
depends upon
its upbringing
only the trained eye
can tell
if a particular
colour
has slummed it,
which is relevant
if modes
of sensibility
are to be one and plastic
in a cityscape

II   *darkness*

come on
any shrink
will tell you
a relationship
needs darkness

consistently
breaking up the
fields of blue/
that's what gives it
its multi-dimensional
character,
that's what makes
our sex-life intere
sting

the white door frame
is an arch
that's angst
in your every move,
come on, loosen up

III *Yellow Manifesto*

at the moment
of perception
the image
is kinetic
pulses
its way
from
one side
of the brain
to the other
almost yellow
on a clear night
the city lights
distant
blue

IV *and the floor fell away*

and the floor fell away
reversing itself
though not quite a reflection

an illusion hints
at a mirror quality
while never being so gauche
as to admit it

or that's what they say
when they look out from the centre
at us looking ...
ad infinitum/
enthusiasm
is colour

V *no vacancies*

there is no room for metaphor
when space is occupied by itself

VI *beauty*

through the coloured glass
you are   indeed   beautiful
maybe the same applies to me

VII *reception*

there is something wrong with the reception
there is no sound
or a warm sound in a blue field
that cannot be heard

VIII *in defence of Velázquez*

Velázquez
take heart
this is op art
so at last
your painstaking
portraiture

has got us somewhere
Velázquez
take heart
there's room in here
for all of us/
space
takes space
(the cover of a book)
for what it is
take heart Velázquez
take heart

On Andy Warhol's *Baseball*
and *Gold Marilyn Monroe*

Marilyn a gold shrouded satellite
orbiting the American Dream, course

marked *collision*: the industrial might
of the nation pre-packed and Fort Knox poised

to catch the shrapnel should the hitters slip.
Re-runs of greatness start to look the same,

but you, Marilyn, retain your aura:
from the earthly DiMaggio, loaded

and ready to leap from the black bunker,
to your heavenly lips, icons worshipped

by every team, loved even in defeat.
And the celebrity pitching the first

ball of the season calls the atmosphere
sweet. The President licks your golden feet.

On Andy Warhol's *Marilyn Six-Pack*

Rip top lips – the movement is piracy.
An early cut – an addict's selective

disclosure. A perfect pose concealing
popular truths, the value of trashy

synthetic polymer makeup, canvas
skin and silkscreened hair. A six-pack's hazy

suppression of class and style, like seeing
the world in black and white. Quick! Look at me!

it pleads with a fizzing hiss. If you stand
long enough success will expose itself.

The pout shapes the plates, but the eyelids take
the weight – suspended languidly below

the constructed eyebrows. O Marilyn –
six tabs without the blister packaging.

On Andy Warhol's *Optical Car Crash*

Movement behind the scene: no rescue can be
a complete success if there's no heartbeat

to be felt, if desolation of metal and flesh
are the motivating factor behind the picture,

if police care only that it might bring sense
to those hitting the gas pedal after a dozen

martinis at the office party. But here, motion
is heartbeat, though irregular and obviously

exposed to death (short polymer green, highly
sugared long-dried-blood red) in the painted

cardiograph. No Marilyn here. But it's nothing
to do with squeamishness or bad publicity. As

Andy realised, she'd a lot to do elsewhere.

On Warhol's *Marilyn Monroe's Lips* and *Red Disaster*

Curse the attractiveness of the cheery
and stereotyped lushness of her lips –

the glam trap – eager – strapped tight to the moist
rollercoaster, a twitch like electric

fleas, a pout that has you bursting with a
shout outwardly bright, well fed; the spirit

just what it should be, and fluorescent teeth –
fit for an advertisement – capture and

isolate the *feminine*, like a flash
billboard – you've got to press a kiss on hers.

Red kills overkill. Expect it. Not just
pink around the gills but ripe on the love

spot. And the doctrine forms the shadow – dark
the lining of her lips, the empty chair.

A 1963 *Lavender Disaster* and Andy Warhol

The satellites were peaches
waiting to be bruised.
                    NAT FINKELSTEIN

The body a peach with its lavender
aura, the executioner synthetic

and imported duty free. The stage-craft
altar industrial and formatted.

Lavender disaster sucked dry dry dry
by the cold room and frame of an electric

chair – witnesses to a disaster pan
frame by frame the knee-jerk reaction, jolts

of pop conscience amongst the share-holders
of destruction: the vinyl balloons filling

the rooms of the Factory. The victims
– chic society claims – will play minor

parts anyway – mere satellites to the
colortones, a lavender celebrity.

On Warhol's *Tunafish Disaster* and *Red Elvis*

Did a leak kill Mrs Brown? Did a leak
kill Mrs McCarthy? Did Elvis chill

out when faced with their cool bodies, eyelids
drooping, while he, with blurred vision could see

with thirty-six sets of eyes, still lusting
after the days when lithium was a

258

tasty table salt? Or when Dick Nixon
relied on him to set the kids straight and

the FBI struck a deal to make all
pink cadillacs bleed like tuna: trusted

icons of supermarkets, suspended
in seas of air-conditioning? Elvis

gently sings the victims in their long sleep,
his red hair as slick as publicity.

On Warhol's *Blue Electric Chair* and *Statue of Liberty*

Low energy? Uh? Partial exposure
to liberty. Andy inside the grand

ol' lady, a Frenchy: like Citroën – be
free and prosper, the market looks after

its own. Nat might take a photo later.
Some years later. Low energy makes for

maximum output – pop equation. Could
be the column of a nuclear ex-

plosion. Rise up like blue washed flame from the
chair. Souvenirs: water on the floor con-

ducting feet towards heaven. Maybe they
bury the victims of pop upside down?

Or blow the whistle on those who throw the
switch. Here, liberty lights the fuse and lives.

The Humble Gents Social Club/*Mustard Race Riot*

> *The thing is that, Andy growing up where he grew up, you would have*
> *expected him to feel more at ease with the poor kids. Thinking of the*
> *hours and hours he would spend talking to all the University-kids that*
> *came to interview him ... with the egg-heads it was FEEL ME, TOUCH*
> *ME, with the slumkids it was YOU'RE BLACK, STAY BACK!*
>
> NAT FINKELSTEIN

Looks like they've got a collective skin
disorder – a problem with pigment. Blank

television screens absorbing all shades,
obliterating technicolor – the

director dragging a lazy stare from
his rubbish bin vantage point. The slumkids

growing bored – art in the making. Move fast
as a mustard Alsatian bites the hand

that doesn't feed it and mustard police
grow confused – Hey! You're supposed to be black

son! Cut them! Check the colour of their blood.
Blah blah blah. But protect yourselves – never

know what's up their dirty sleeves. Poor Andy.
Gotta get him back to the Factory.

Diamond Dust Joseph Beuys à la Andy Warhol

Diamond Dust Joseph Beuys – silkscreen ink
and diamond dust on synthetic polymer paint
on canvas equivocates beneath his spiritual
hat, motivation lifting him out of darkness,
chemi-luminescent or infrared or just rich.

Morris Graves's *Blind Bird* Is Given Sight

I

Blind
it would have sat
on the window sill
without second thought,
now it stares at its feet
for hours, sometimes lifting
one, balancing for a while
and then settling again. Beyond
the open window is freedom.
But it doesn't look
for solutions to questions
that must have arisen when blind.

II

The choice
of darkness
is always there
but now it has to keep
an eye out for itself. The window
is still open, and it is looking
out and cocking its head and opening
its wings, but something in the way
it scrunches its eyes closed
says that darkness was preferable.

III

Sometimes
I think that
it is not comfortable
with the world as revealed –
not so much out of shock,
as disappointment. But at night
when moonlight touches
its beak I can
almost see it smile.

IV

Today
it sang a song
I've not heard
since it was blind

and it took some seed
and drank a little water.
Tomorrow, it might fly,
I feel that even this
is possible.

V

It was gone
when I went to check
this morning.

I wouldn't worry
but there was a storm
last night. The carpet
at the foot of the window
is wet, and there are
branches down in the yard.

I slept soundly.

I wouldn't worry
but the darkness
was so sweet to it,
and with the storm

it may have lost
this final joy,
the confusion
destroying
its last refuge.

Helen Frankenthaler's *Interior Landscape*, 1964

The window frame – contained –
breaks out, into darkness,
                    the darkness of cupboards
                                linen presses
                                cellars and lofts

something projects
                    and takes sunrise or sunset
and breeds an aura – breath –
about the interior   space
                            light thinning
the clouded sight

                    *What do you suggest? That we
move these things over here? the precipice is clear,
and the bridge looks safe.*

a couple sit, the child takes centre stage
and outgrows them
                    now, the footholds are few
and deceptive
            *Look dear, there's a field of deep green
in the living room ...*

                    the child gone, they fear an exterior
will occupy and consume.

Sappho Paints Sappho

I

Everywhere
fields are brazen
with harvest,
even harsh ground
is rich

and everywhere
people are strong –
labourers, land-owners,
all share the season's health

But why is it
that from amongst
this flush of life
we commit to memory

the pale face
of a thin girl
gritting her teeth
as she ties a sheaf?

II

DESIRE

Desire shakes me once again,
here is that melting of my limbs.
It is a creeping thing, and bittersweet.
I can do nothing to resist.
                    trs. SUZY Q. GRODEN (1964)

The painting
is without centre –
it is empty
though maybe we imagine
a cool evening,
a lilac sunset
and an aroma

of brooding citrus
spilling into the room

the frame tells us more –
it is spattered in colours
often considered comfortable –
pastels, soft blues

a number of cushions
seem to float
in an arc, or maybe
this is an early moon;
suffice it to say
there is something
tempting here,
that there
will be love
no matter what
we'd like to think

III

THE ORCHARD

Cold water falls between the appletrees
And climbing roses over-arch their shade,
And rustling in the leafy boughs the breeze
Lulls every sense.

trs. A.R. BURN (1965)

There are plumes of smoke
in the background, rising
from the sea – possibly
ships burning, a volcano
forming. The foreground is
lush though indistinguishable –
colour shimmer, the surface
could even be glass. Love
and pigment ground in the
mortar and pestle of vanity.
Shades fill the background,
lulling the senses – the
breeze pressing the sea,
content with itself.

On Kenneth Noland's *Turnsole*, 1961

Turnsole, underfoot
and in crudest terms
(it must be said) targeted.
Emblematic, lost
in a willingness to be seen
concrete and real
though politely magnificent
when the brand name
        is lifted.
Turnsole, trapped in the space
of your own making, not a pulsating
Universe, this is steel-hooped
and indelible, the Universe
precisely ninety-four and one eighth of an inch
by ninety-four and one eighth of an inch,
        flat, made of canvas,
                acrylic.

A Page on Balthus

Balthus, as represented here
in three black and white reproductions
and two short paragraphs, is caught
on the edge of something. As you said
this afternoon, the potential is in everyone –
in *The Street* the business of each figure
is self-contained though necessary
to the esprit de corps, the mood centres
on the scene's balance. In *Portrait
of André Derain*, it would seem the model
has been wasted by Derain's constant approaches:
robed, hand on heart, he fills the foreground
with presentiment – a red herring – it is
the model who one night will awaken
from her doll-like sleep, repel the dream
of his thick eye and sharp hand
from her legs, and plunge a knife
deep into his breast. And in *The Living Room*
a dream is as good as anxiety, the tablecloth
lifted like the hem of a skirt, a love
story's sweet words drawing knees to chest,
the cat scowling, the divan inviting
Balthus to whisper carefully to himself.

On Susan Rothenberg's *Red Banner*, 1979

Red Banner, bone-wrap,
skin flag, bloody flier,
they shoot horses don't they?

Nuptial joke, a buck's party,
the saddlebag strung side-saddle,
pony express, weary eyes run into flesh.

The tao arrested, it's not polite
to do it in public. Drum taps on hide
sinew-wound, taut on its frame. A court martial.

A bison on a cave wall erupts
as the flash captures its spirit.
'Emblematic,' says the student. It's not a bison.

And this isn't a horse, nor
the bones of a horse. The black
is the armour, the white a naked body.

Red banner, bone-wrap,
skin flag, bloody flier,
they shoot horses don't they?

Lilith Spies on Adam And Eve

The artist Arthur Boyd
was granted a vision:

he watched an angel
watching Adam and Eve kissing

he watched as a ram at their feet
watched back, remaining silent

he watched as a deformed
nightjar elevated itself

on thinning legs and pretended
to go about its business.

It did not cross the angel's mind
that his robes had been consumed

by the soft blood that comes halfway
from the heart, that Paradise

was glowing with the embers
of his trance, smouldering

with the passion of Eve's hair, Adam's
desperate grip on her bare back;

nor did it occur to him
that Lilith may have been

instigating her riot from beneath
his cloth, between the eyes of the ram

and the observations of a nightjar
so effectively disguised.

Beyond Paul Klee's *Death and Fire*

Puffer fish with head wounds
sink into the riverbeach, wrapped
in ashen froth. The lower deck
of the jetty disappears beneath
grey waves, the river absorbs
and then indulges. This,
the aftermath of the 'hottest
day on record', the oppression
of logic as the clouds brood
thickly against the heat.
The water guards against
a crossing, an early star
sparks three times and vanishes.
Death and fire, the season
drowns in its own blood.
Extreme, restless, the river
casts back fire rolling down
from parks and gardens, tears
at the moorings (old engine
blocks) of cruisers, yachts,
and ferries. There is fire
and death on its breath.

SYZYGY

(1993)

1   Apprehension

And how did you feel
the surface too close
and the flappers fizzing
at your tender
and vulnerable
                feet
loaded with misgivings?
Swift overload catapulting
recrimination
the largess culminating
cinema papers boys-own-annual-ing
from post office to mailbox
and bicycle-clip braces
on the maligned bull terrier's
teeth: an island of green
reticulated sucked into the soft pink
of the suburb, insurmountable the ratepayer's
anguish and bravado! the house a kraken
or bathysphere undercutting the plane,
adjunct to surface, one dimensional
suction. O fear ripples evading
sonar buoys Blue Gum Lake
receding as bores suck effluent
from beneath the arses of ducks.

Paperbarks turn black
water soils over
banks of sodden bread
and soft drink cans
this is popular viewing
medium small frame minutiae
chronic screen or inhabited pasture,
pointillist and contentious
cartooning serious ineptitudes
hatchback unravelling a bend
the lock-stock
barrelling it into sticky drink
at the bottom of the can: sure,

we feel strung up and depleted – light
even heavy and darkness uplifting,
necessitating remission into screaming
as the engine revs the flywheel
seems not to move dear o dear
love's texts spread haphazardly over the bucket
seats – and don't we know
they're braggarts! denying fusion
and invading asteroids, deploying
consumables and calling
it art.

2 Fallout

A refugee from contention I load
stills into the projector
taking the negative impression
adjuncting
expression prising anger
out of its folds
the damage budding retentive
small experiment releasing heat:
remember looting these impressions?
machinery expressive and light-
conscious love scarifying poise
the tractor rocketing the clods of loamy earth
bootlegging frustration mudbrick and fencewire
circular-saws threatening Robert Frosts
and doorpost jamming two years too old
and rotting, the sun orange plastic,
perfect, the film was black
and white and the sheep gurgling
hysterically.

3   Self-regard

-ing homunculus metals chambers
tinfoiling exclusions like humidicribs
wheeling slick asphalt deletions
and stripping film, dust water licking
axminster carpet spreadsheets – what shows
in the headlights or pinheaded
spotlight? Crunch. Synthetic victims.
And the frogs croak politely
in their ditches. HALT! Good year
wet weather halts the death of a zebra
just outside a butcher's shop. Can't read the signs
good who gives a damn anyway?
Needed, inquire within: good management
and sensible market indicators.
Those who leave anything up to description
need not remote opinions. Morality
stinks, we keep it in buckets.

4   When the flappers tickle your fancy

opposing needs, priming pellegra
with plastic cement like jelly rubber
singing aging movies, tall tales lugging drabness
out of forums: humitrophic, water glass
or sundial gas-bagging in the shade, Ah
such is fame passing the time. The car comes.
A stretch in tails. Silk doors predella
adjuncting talent AND the driver. Let us in!
Take us entire rhomboidal all and Oolala
susurrous through disconnexion, baffling
sibilance. O my flappers, what a team we make!
And the planets co-habitate and read life
impression, you have your strict

and your lax, the cups drink too much
and the television in the back of the limo
is stuck on the same channel. The driver
is sucking himself. Take no notice.
You are my family he splurges:
executors   guardians   trustees
receivers   inheritors
good sides half backs
flankers absorbers potentates
contrivers emissaries
agitators incarnations
lovers leaping onto the tired pile
of my flesh.

5   The Cane Cutter

Reflex take a breath.   ( )   A snake
operates amongst rough cane-cutter's crystalline sweat.
A particle overload.
Heavy rain bearing down
palpitating trifolate with sun and cane
no rainbow
makes an appearance.
Earthy very earthy. Miasma
camouflaged mud takes all takers
and throws back a marsh of fences.
They beg for tariffs. They like restrictions.
In the highlands water is lightning
gaping press-down and half bas-relief.
Turbine churn-out comes down
from highlife where the air is heady.
No fireflies there. Dowsed and riddled
deep deep south roots dry the bone-black
subterranean streams, raddled shapes forking azurine
on meeting archaeological light, spent swarming
the traps, for this is Ground Zero Warholing
in cyclone territory, zoning the sirens
equivocating hot dogs and pies mushrooms

pushed to the side of the plate: cadillacs
racketing Monroe hubcaps
currency cut like love
on a breezy day, hot air concentrating
in the sewers.

6 Life-driver

Placating pit swimmers
the bone mill splurgers
credit cards bursting middle-class prognosis
dialectic good will and science
is upon us bursting prognosis
good will tragacanth
imprint forms lotus form
the new behemoth, a signature naked
beneath the ultra-violet: rex regis
suppressing atoll watchers, spreading
blood and bone over the garden. Lair-down devil
lair down! Vrooom!

7 Subjecting objects to serious scrutiny

Draining absence as blue
trance stelazine melting circulars
            restraining the abstract
            fingerpainting
lithium to bind
Mono Mondrian on its platform of shape:
threatening construction on its very
printed page, corrector fluid

swashbuckling first words
formatted like a river ending
in a window mouse decorating
graphic disasters
without compassion. We impose.
Macrographic–Beta–Language.
And you don't even have to
drop names!
                    Advertising blimps
nudge traffic controllers pneumatic
in their agitating seats,
tattoos green with red tracers
running like hits. Here, disasters
falsetto screech *sus. per coll.*
like corporate suicide
across the polished screens.

8   The forest, the farm. a hybrid bathysphere

Lumped or polyglotted, mixing
but insistent on claustrophobic
limits, cans of repellent
stink like flypaper.
They undercut a fluid market
holding back the fragile forest,
rending tight-as-money-talk, marketeers
would cut sleepers where they stood:
Chinese whispers like nostalgia. Downburnt
the weird beast charts pressure, breath
contrivance as the water is fire:
volunteers roll back the pasture, the forest
corals and suffers. Greenhousing
the coldest waters, peepshow languishing
amongst saw-jawed lantern fish
surface molten, stripped of its cage.

9 Inflecting ambiguity / electric trains

A type of ambiguity
that carves the hissing wires
clouds volcanic on the scarp
as kids general motor it with a mania
that drives them East: surveillance
a seance partially materialising
voices from closets steel-faced
and never changing critics
like having a field day: tracks glisten
briefly like sin in its rage
cauterising
           rugged–up patrons waiting
for concert tickets outside
the entertainment centre
as staunch pylons share goods and flashes
with cameras and country trains, not electric
but still photogenic. Dispensation
of tickets as curricles dash past
and we celebrate the past.

10 Palpable Paludal – the defence rests

Palpable cacology – admit the document –
juggling heartburn
passing paludal intoxicants
adhesives and cleansing agents
out back the hardware store
supermarket strings strummed or struck
the plastic shopping bag dissolving
or blowing up like a lung,
thick and tumorous when breath whispers
triplicate super realist on super realist
zygal chevron zippered–up
the fire-escape rusted

and decompressed – the blossom
plucked while locked
in its cloak and cap, night-fruit
copping it sweet in daylight: our bodies
botanical: façades
as the tallest poppy
accepts the flak
its tinted window reflecting
it back, carbonaceous angels
triggering sumptuous sprinklers,
the housing estates sinking
into the swamp stomping
faddish death beats
only the well-heeled speak
borrowing cultural tid-bits
repackaged   tender   taste-sensitised
suppressing the threats.

11 Deletions

Fortitude rippling cross-sense-
a-round clip-board logic
accumulating detailing Harleys
like shepherd's calendars in the month
of January the heat was Cyrenaic and intense
displaced vermilion weathering
irregularities like windows
and quick assimilations, pique & niche,
lavender disaster soft and not in the slightest
mechanical – BUT deletion rakes
a monster making shape from less
than its constituents, well-made enigmas
propitiatory hermeneutic and well coded,
I differ camping on fault-lines highways upending
bridges siphoning rivers neuter
crushed velvet ripped from the dash,
die bobbing infra-red night sight slick like bedrock and pylons
congealed beneath town planners forgetting mud, acronym

comfortable city lazy body lay-about
the pool pretzels beer and much more: the 'staff of life'
single tracking compression and tidiness,
an accident absorbs clumping only
for publicity: obliquity luxuriant
first class dozer drivers machining silver spray
amyl nitrate staining fingers
in tills corporate gets-ya-goin' up and adam
furrowing nutrition and filling cavities.

12   Entropy / Flesh

Spontaneous bloodstock rattles and broods
lapping power-lifted pasture amidst
the fences — narcs and passive devourers of feed
immunising syringes. Meathood gestures gantries
and ramps while Soutine feeds love in a French
abattoir la la la B grade and trendy, rattle O three-tiered
calashes, looking brutal in the halogens, cauterising
debris up-ended white posts with red and silver
dazzlers lowering their lids, slipping on damp days
into the smell of wool and hide, mopping
placental blankets with rough tongues.
Window painting stretch addressing
ambulance and attendant starter motors
commensural commercial additives
like bolt guns stunning and electro-shock
on top of the hill beneath a liver-shaped moon
draining the blood from your nervous
system-ism, the spill-down lathering
the coronets of your contact-lenses, drainage inquiline
wearing it like a glove or
coating stomachs – STIFFEN UP LADS! the Hoi
polloi tax-evading and avoiding road-blocks
born into banking liquids that solidify
with limb-movement, the floor
approaching rapidly: a Gnostic

logion: the fish nibbles my toes
and good it feels sovereign vessels toes & lips
divisive
hobnobbing
traipsing stainless on the whetstone   outcrop
sheep-weather-alert
or battery-bound and the wind chafing tinwalls
clocking the pulse of eggdrop and peelable wool
and udders performing ridiculous labours: supreme-O
a brand name marketable, affirmations corporate
conferring garnished parsley hints, staking
first grade glue sticks how many shares?
brokered on the floor household cleansers
banish the addictive canvas, Ah tundra vista
the canvas captures and projects
the sky shocked and hooked
Mrs McCarthy & Mrs Brown
immobilised by Tuna fish, disaster spread
like emulsified stabilised sheen upon
Marilyn's tender lips c/- Big Sirs: Sir
of the pigskin briefcase, brylcream quinella
stated portfolio lapses pump-action
and blood-staked, entablature
en-loading your own quizzing sense-around. Smell it!
Singing western and roto broiling I've hooked a big one
bone black and threatening to move
quotes like numerous grains of dry powder
centrefire monumentalised 1080
vacuuming heat-sealed trophies skins
pre-packaged mise-en-scène urging texture
out of quadrature, arc the brittle black
cuttlefish, sepia toning cinemas
flensing storage facilities, you drag
something up out of memory and into sight.
Steaming black frost cleansing sun deliciously sharp
and breakfasting on the damp patio, lush tallow
candle canopying shades and predicting a good
hard-humping sunset. Progenate policedog
physiology derived and detecting goals
evaluating hereditary from 'weaning to slaughter'
heterozygous random carcass the beauty
collapses, Santayana might have been ugly.

13 Ripples

Streaming blue divisions, sections
of the neighbourhood, the lights of Canning Vale
ludicrous sporting brilliance rainslicks
like the MCG and gracing a stadium of cages –
Movietone ships sink and planes disperse
in black strategy, walk-on parts erotically
developing & reproducing cryptic typologies;
passion active and unassailable, declaring
intermittently, rippling like the skin
of persons or sulo-bins rattled by traffic,
city initiated carnivale for officers
on chilly Autumn nights eking out nostalgia
clumped together at the same scene long after
the bang, roadgame, cosmic microwave
background radiation as the fighter plane
sends tracers spitting into columns
of uniformly spread refugees: organisation
saves none of them.

14 Trigger

Yoke the vicious integer, sun and moon
uncomfortably syzygetic: 'Deep Throat'
shifting consensus, plead your case
and get the hell out of here. I won't
listen anyway! The quadrature sets limits
AND appeals X pronto. Things don't stick
unless they're forced to. No couples
can sit comfortably here: rekindling
love-on-a-pier, the car humming
on a verge or aiming for the country
downwind and forgetful upending the heart
off-loading blots of anger a clock chimes
in a mall of pastiche. Trigger, I fall
collecting apogean multiples of disorder.

15   Landfall / The Collapse of Beauty

Loose materials patterning sundials
at water's edge: embracing saline
trend/'/s crystalline fatigues
–loss– myriad system
–is–ation
interest vis à vis
disintegral compendiums, oil-slick
& refuse & foam casually concocting
beneath an historic swing bridge
a couple of hours [drive fro]m Perth, up-river
skiers hacking the lower
reaches
and paddocks might appear
mostly folds of beauty
– tourists understand this! – satisfying
rare inner-city creatures marooned
passive purposeful indulgently
headlines might claim.

16   Chemical

Boom-arm pod-fed nuzzles teaming foam
out over red earth: new machines
churning chemical seas in-lateral drift-a-round
phenomenally hand-in-hand with tractors
and deranged furrows rippling
heavy clods of soil
                              run-off creek river sea
deranged furrowing residual
        when myth hits purchase
who wants clean food?
bulimic south anorexic mid-point
        dr i p-fed north
deep-inhaling flyspray
and mosquito coils

fr - ie - ze dried coffee
cleaning a particularly
stubborn stove or bad guests
from a party.

17   First Blood

Tubed out of you warm and recycled cold.
Flow impedes logic cold as stain-
less steel like a disinterested object
of beauty, sun-bathing internal solarium
blood ultra'd & raddled
re: transfusion. Dizzy float extract
inflatables, double toxicological
cell-sized machines making repairs
restructuring walls disengaged
by injective inter-ex-change
blood money breathes
franchise fantastic voyage
efficient redistribution
for this they test. byo.
branching profusely
gaining the respect
of ambulance drivers
slamming T-bar automatics gloved
and averting, petrol-guzzling
monsters finned and beautiful
gybing through your sanguine &
unguent utterings
staunch against venomous
        '{Dais de l'œil revulse}'
bathe five death on red/s: (a) disaster
guilt feud bath (h)ound letting lust sport
thirsty money-stained sucker
auspicate consanguinity
rarely colourless or violently positive
genealogy suppurating

my grandfather fell
into the offal pit: Benny's Bonemill
      circa
1923.

18   peine forte et dure

What pleads 'I',
in the gloom, of
bulb-blow
& ocean-carpet
closing shore
lee & lea
to hills
a sprinkle of desquamating quartz
     sun-dank
spent
             re-flex-ive
though who owns the fragments (?)

19   Gloat

who   lives by
  lies by
and
buy re-active blood/y
mis-fortune
assigned Con tra Dik shuns
an audience despite their buying
   him drinks
pneumatics taxonomy dialectics
   & quark of despair.

20 Feedback

Charles (O)lson
'Not one death but memor
   ot accumulation but change, the feedback is
the   aw

21 Fume

Soil tactless infuses
dust-cradles   *   objectifies
black frost on breathing land
fuming. anger military
pro fuse   Ion deficient
upper upper   flight
developing a dislike
for 'us': the bulldozers
have sweet tooths & fume.

22 Float – ing

I

Respond
float-ing soil
heresy
and the fog
absorbs pink-quartz
thrust-drift.

II

Tractor churns heavy
despotic bones: sheep anatomy
undering edgy discs
and salty furrows luminous
night-work
driver's red-neck hurts.

III

Fencing wire coils
snakes complex
in gullies

crops
and wild radishes
rot.

IV

Scour stalk-base and stubble
vast rimmed fields
charred in waves,
ash-water lapping
like gout: first rains
float.

23   Narrative

I   *telescope: passive*

Up in the hills / closer: week (end) tours
not the building you'd think
[though] they've made
the right moves in the foyer. The
predicate fails to leave, we assume
via adjustin gth efoca llen g th
that he's always been (t)here! Zeiss
optics.

II *the night sky might be an all day sucker*

take down [to] flatlands the jigger
of nostalgia – a few slides lo-priority
& secure. they call him Kid. hey Kid
cop a load of the moon} loud in his
ear pricking with chilly air. it & the sun.
orange & blue.
his father's hand conjoin-
ing
with an ear
left spare.

III *the living planet*

seeder/combine. re-building
rain-washed spreads. the water deleterious & demi.
And all they've got to say
Is what a wonderful vista!
Not city lights absorbing
The stars – even the moon
Looks (more) vivid. Taut.   here
Check out sun in summer's

                                   centre
Comes the reply. I'll bet ya!
Cannot [any] lies well in randomness?

IV *Expansion*

lock stock and barrel
ie carrying its orbit in-
consistently.   Note: key words. access?
Proper
bucketing
they gave him.
Proper. and they've electrified the railway
as well.
what the hell, he drank his first wine
at communion. transfixed: Kid's re-
call.

288

23 Na(rra)tive / chapelle ardente

Syz-23-key: uh oh
fetish or frou-frou
aza labels & ers on
artifize the case:
richter's rats struggle
& quickly
give up: identify. musical casing
setted. Up up up!

Rhe
-toric plans an
invest   atations & calendars: grey
gunboats sweeping
dank rainforest rivers. patrons
of calypse & stoker
the moon drums UP tides: awash
melt-in-the-mouth} riprap.
& drawn out. ra ra ra.

isotopies
Id di
poussières
gestes
temps perdu tristan tzara
morphemic and trendy
up-
wards & categorise?

linger
mechaniser
'senex iratus'
swiftly
sits: progression towards
a system. Yes.
Yes.

logos
go go
& presuppose a % of
an   *

[vraisemblance]
eschews a?

Touchy on a point
of picture & linkage = so what?
newstart with a kick
& get comfortable.

This case has potential: look,
they've got the drop
on you. De-
tailing
edifice &
scripture/s &
inspire-
ation: the sun brightens
          the shell grouting
          paving the lap lap
          of motoring stretched
          waves & sandbar circumflexed
          the pillars softly set
          and sinking, coming unstuck
          on soft-served banks, upwards
          & downwind the puckered hills
          glow like the haze. A fly
          settles on a fish corpse
and dies.

23.5   Pantoum

souwester blows cold
ha ha says granma
you'll chill to the bone
out there on the water

ha ha says granma
we gotta anyway
out there on the water
that's where goes sun & moon

we gotta anyway
cold when it oughta be hot
that's where goes sun & moon
burst & mix with blue

cold when it oughta be hot
we saw it in the telescope
burst & mix with blue
burnt dark like the road

we saw it in the telescope
granpa let us look
burnt dark like the road
& too close to lie

23   Lift

Ex hale and don't re-
(in) flate
                  it's dark
when you go out
{ing}   the fires
retract wetlands
breathe iced lakes
spoonbill & ibis
lurch–dance (in) space
{ing}   monograms
   [memory] re-
call the day, the weight
of light–lift, roll-back
sun buoyant
sienna-&-orange   luff & clouds & hills
obsessive and
manic   *   prone to out-
bursts
de rigueur
Ah! not love neat on the bus

I see {thru} your window/face
             take
me back.

24   On

Oh ON!   loosely
never held   pivot(al) sans
      desire
on degeneration c/- object in
NO! touch me. On.

25   Urban Cross-over

Your soy-coloured teeth
moth dust skin dys
function
-al: redress:
just a question
of supply: all roads lead in,
supply: all your
working daze: shopping trolleys
con-joining
in car-
parks. Howzat?

26 Rural Patronising

Trill & twee wagtail lift
little nervous
nell-ies
take a break
at the heart the header
moves out over good soil
rippling like radiation
an electric
storm
spiriting
up-lifts,
& the fear
of fire & need for rain.

27 Intermission

I chase a hair
over my lip
trace it
with
tongue
& shiver spine deep and
hear my insides
recoil: a glass
to the wall!

28 Reality

If it's real it's been photo-
graphed but not by lips
testing on recall cauterised
word(s) – slash & burn, scorched
earth realising opacity
of skin and smooth cool sight
in our hands, wounds
washed & THE LAND
never sulking.

29 Link

Speech I link. Pro–
crastinate. 'Weialala leia'. Eh?
What did you say?
Can't make
head nor tail.
Of it: lyric?

30: re (con) str<u>uctur</u>e ing / damage
control

(a) *Ponge c/– or à la Fahnestock*

ah
'In this undergrowth, half shade half-sun
Who thrusts these sticks between our spokes?'

river white burnt & scullcraft
taunting drift downtide, down
in the mouth & down towards
the centrifugal drag, & towed
& motored the sherry stained
ramps, I cry & laugh and palpitate

& can

not right & moralise
& catastrophise & lies
out & about before sequestering
downs the spout & closes
the ment (al) gap: lash
out

                              no longer & yet
locate a shell of me like paving stones
zippy brass em[boss]-ing names
but not mine
god
willingly
the swells of pleasure lurid
& not a little jealous
of another era

                    seventy miles from here
                    where on lordly manors

clean hope
for forgiveness
but no more
blood below hook & rafter
becoming dirt

but
no more
cast in plaster
moulded joan   of arc   or jocaster
in revolutionary colours
caged & carved
                    biblical
red velvet fierce companions
perfect
eyes are missing
cont-
            rol is
or has   been
dam(ag)ed:

quartz or nacre
lose lustre (less)
minutiae
packed & labelled
analytic & rolling
    fencewire
plugging gulleys

certain
even

       lichen covered rags
scrunched & welded
ARE dead parrots
sauve-qui-peut
  (!)

The point of impact
fabricates & inde
pend {ates} enhances – a disc plough
or slave cylinder
mixing mediums
with disaster
intra-personally: saltwash,
the creeks are storming
the river
& the crops are
waterlogged – melaleuca & salt scars
collaborate in a bundesfest
discordant
visits politely
call ING music
out-back. the tractor   ['wends its weary way]
no longer bushbashing
but suppurating spray
from soil, frisking
clean air
& tourists
warm in town

                    (as
                    Uncle Gerry
                    talks to Les Murray
                    who compares
                    Bunyah with

pasture
& a trio
of harmonists
make a go of friendship
without a tenor
providing a damn good
afternoon tea. You won't hear
cheques bouncing here. rather
sinking sand
& cockatoos.

& yes, we can hear the shutters
a-clicking & the chortle
of buses cruising down
the town's main street.

a stickler in a yella rain-jacket checkin'
the water troughs out in the rain
always wishing more sheep shelter
& the precise quantity & placement
of precipitate, as the tractor
sidles up to the silver fuel tank
& drinks.
this, I know. & re-
lease. the tractor is a star!
out here.

hot lead is introduced
to Crater Valley. Not True valley,
more of a deep deep creek between granite
and sandstone sweeps & high language shot & sheeted. crumble
lipping down to the York Gummed floor
& sheets split as sharp
as plough discs. of course.
For Crater Valley is also
The Valley of Foxes.
& they come, cousins & weekend hunters
& deplete.
& the need for locusts
as the third bell is raised
in its tower & God spits yellow
is begrudgingly ac-

cepted.

& earth-tear
(as) families quake
stationwagons, earth snake
deep down & ripping up

298

| Alien |

hatchling.   old barn down
and (the) wells drained:
fresh gullies
ground thunder

groundwater thunders (complete)

despair
backstroking cross-lane or cutting the windrows
of THE childhood nightmare   I look
to the STREET
for a % -age & Age
& free (of)
tracasseries/   replete

(b)   *& Ponge / Fahnestock:*

        'As also for
grass to straw,
or to the calamus for writing

to the pipe of 'inspiration'
(…and to the straw in the 'cocktail',
in the tall glass of the 'long drink')'

&

the '&' is OUR angel.

Eh, balance up
spreadsheet
& paint on the carpet,
selling out
& making my almost (self)
<clear>. Eh, SPEAK UP
with subtlety:
I'm here & your practising virtue.

Eh, SPEAK UP
I can't hear & listen too quickly:

> he shook the box
> and could NOT
> guess the contents.

Tractor parts.
Splinters from
THAT wagon wheel.
& a copy
of

POETRY

|M a r c h   1 9 6 6

Mary Ellen Solt: 'Flowers In Concrete'
'Magnificent
Aureoles
Rousing
Insensate
Grief
Oh
Long
Death
Suddenly'   #   here bottlebrush trees
drag blood out of cemeteries.

WIRELESS HILL

(1992-1994)

Skippy Rock, Augusta: Warning, the undertow

1

Oystercatchers
scout the tight rutilic
beach, rust charting

run–off locked
cross–rock up–coast
from the bolted

lighthouse
where two oceans
surge & rip & meet.

2

Immense the deep lift
seizes in gnarls & sweeps,
straight up & built

of granite. A black
lizard rounds & snorts
the froth capillaried

up towards dry–land's
limestone, hill–side
bone marrow mapped

by water. Meta–wrought,
the lighthouse distantly
elevates & turns

the crazily
bobbing history
of freak waves

and wrecks: wrought iron
& lead paint brewing
deep in capsized

sea lanes, talking shop
in thick clots of language,
bubbles thundering topwards.

3

The stab holes
of fishing poles,
small-boy whipping

those gate–
crashing waves releasing
shoals of wrecked

cuttlefish bleeding sepia
like swell prising
the weed-swabbed rocks

& darkly crescented beach:
crabclaw & limpet
scuttlebutt

about the rubbery
swathes of kelp.
Tenebrous lash

& filigreed canopy
of dusk-spray, undertow
of night.

Rushcutters' Bay

1

Should we peel back the foil
That blackens a second surface?
The sun as intent as the harmonics
Of waves layering the festive craft,
The tunings of masts and metal ropes,
The way people seem to intend strangers
To hear their most intimate secrets.
Jugglers hone interplanetary skills
On manicured lawns as water taxis
Sweep in for the kill, the dynamics
Of body language as cool sailors
Let their boats moor themselves.

2

Out there the naval dockyard, sun-
Blind, becomes a whale struck like the blunt
Rump of the continent, huge dead-in-the-water
Dreadnought sun-aged and corroded
Into place, obstinately lined against silent
If darker sailings. Drawn like black flags
When trawlers, docking with their bellies
Full of gutted shark, fly their deadly ensigns;
Or dolphins guide aluminium craft through
The harbour mouth towards the scaling benches,
Runaways slapping the solid water as a Tiger
Moth, wired like a reconstructed fossil, floats
High-pitched & low, brightly overhead.

3

The masts of these yachts lean west
And a forty-footer sidles up to its
Moorings with a look of loss. A light
Breeze flurries from all directions
And begs an explanation. A curlew –
Sitting hunched and filling its eyes –
Might sense you're near without
Showing it. A plastic boom at the mouth
Of a canal holds back urban residue
As fish come in from the sea to feed.
A Bulgarian family works this placid water
Within this placid bay in complex ways.
Hooks and sinkers disappear in black holes
Deep below the surface. Bystanders marvel
At the intricacies of collusion between
Humans and fish, the bay brimming
With its artificial catch of yachts
Which still seem organic (if lithographic)
Against the brooding sunset.

The Jetty Poems
(poems of evapo-transpiration) with Variations etc. in mm & with love

Although no one is without the belief that material things exist, yet because we have just called it into question and counted it amongst the prejudices of our upbringing we must now inquire into the grounds of its certainty.

DESCARTES

The Forsaken River – Variations on a Theme

In a coign of the cliff between lowland and highland,
At the sea-down's edge between windward and lee,
Walled round with rocks as an inland island,
The ghost of a garden fronts the sea.
A girdle of brushwood and thorn encloses
The steep square slope of the blossomless bed
Where the weeds that grew green from the graves of its roses
Now lie dead.

SWINBURNE, 'A Forsaken Garden'

Mt Henry Bridge/Spinaway Crescent

High curving a-spin, the traffic frantic
    Over-head, a-squat, heavy-haunched
The river barely moving, fishing static
    Between the yellow lines, as compacted
Yachts and sparkling cruisers cut past
    Crazy scullers in their second skins,
And teenagers living life loose and fast
    gather sins.

Plunging thirteen metres into the piranhaic
    Drink from platforms frescoed with prawn-
Heads, blood, and vicious hooks in triplicate,
    Their florid leaps destroying the morn-
Ing, Time held under and the river red-purple
    Through lack of breath. So by way
Of relief you let your cinematographic eye settle
    distantly.

One of many possible ends, where long-legged
      Birds stalk the young of flathead and cobbler,
Or, when fully fed, lunge without a shred
      Of decorum amongst the entropic militia
Of stranded jellyfish; where you sit on a jetty
      That is marooned at high tide, accepting
Loss as something to hide: ah, place named lightly
      Spinaway.

From Mount Henry Bridge to Spinaway Crescent

High curving spin on heavy-haunched pillars,
no fishing between the yellow lines

as yachts & pleasure craft cut past
the scullers, & crazy contradictory teenagers

leap or plunge or are pushed by bravado-drunk mates
into the early morning drink. 'Come on, break the ice!'

they say, aiming for the ringleader in his florid under-
wear: the prawn heads, bloodstains, and hooks, between

the yellow lines, conspiring as they drop twelve metres,
live bait, all fed to the piranhaic drink,

For them, & for me – spectator caught in Socratic
tyranny – time is stilled between leap & entry

(though no longer stilled in the perpetual thrill & agony)
as the eye moves towards the dead-end of the river:

mudflats where flathead & cobbler breed quietly
and all waterbirds have overly long & slender legs

& stalk amongst the entropic hulks of stranded jellyfish.
Ah, place named after my brother's first girlfriend's

father's father's houseboat – The Spinaway.
Where light is & sight ends & memory diminishes.

The Forbidden River / Mt Henry Bridge to Spinaway Crescent

High curving & a-spin on heavy haunches, no fishing
      Between the yellow lines as yachts & pleasure
Craft cut past the crazy scullers in their second skins, & feeding
      Contradiction frantic teenagers take a thirteen-metre
Plunge into the piranhaic drink, leaping from a concrete
      Platform frescoed with prawn heads, blood, & vicious hooks
In triplicate, following a big-boned ringleader with discrete
      gasps of fear.

In their florid 'ersatz' they take Time and hold it under
      Far too long, the river purple with its lack of breath,
So by way of relief, your eyes will break free & wander
      To river's end, mudflats where birds-of-stealth
Stalk the young of flathead & cobbler, or when fully fed
      Lunge between entropic hulks of stranded jelly-
Fish. Funny that they named this place after a boat long since dead:
      Spinaway.

Gunbower Road Jetty

Where as a thirteen-year-old boy I was stabbed and thrown,
      My Malvern Star bicycle anchoring me,
The grey-brown water become a permanent stain,
      A dreary vision as indelible as victory.
That grassed banks force you to newly-laid planks,
      And nasturtium flowers reach out towards squat
Buddha pylons, paperbarks – stripped back, agisted in ranks –
      meditate.

And those austere herons disturbed by vandals,
      Hoons in speedboats ignore their damage – the flurry
And dizzy mixing of adrenalin and water as wetsuits gamble
      With an influx of sewage, sauve-qui-peut! Flee!
Bow-wave bodies as viscous as mercury, though words
      Mean nothing and drift sfumato over a picturesque
City. Those heron cope poorly and drag thinly away, most birds
      take no risks.

Lith lith lith against the breeze they refuse to coerce
 In this traffic of words, lips don't move but are overheard.
Between the years the shadows move, lifebuoys ring like a source
 Of verse, and you shoot a glance straight to the river bed
Expecting to be stirred, but water absorbs and distorts,
 As sound transgresses and defines its rite, hissing
As it tunes burley cages lodged between planks, and the rorts
 of fishing.

Deep Water Point 1

In waters punitive as algae blooms,
 Superbly deceptive as the surface
Enhances this crystalline image, fumes
 Of dead fish disperse, distance
Framing the sanitised reflection.
 And so the morning-still jetty
Hides the gross truth, its intention
 met darkly.

Deep Water Point 2

In waters punitive, as algae blooms and slobbers,
 Though superbly reflective on the surface, as distance
Enhances this crystalline image, the jetty gathers
 Its perfect reflection, picturesque in its resistance
To this most grotesque of truths – it is verging on death.
 That gangsters would need no blocks of concrete,
The muddy bottom dragging all down – traces of breath
 darkly met.

Rookwood St Jetty

T-shaped with money to back it up, all Esplanades appeal
    To the upwardly mobile or those with family money,
Camouflaged against the glare & prettified by the river's seal,
    Cruisers moored just a little way out, catamarans lobbying with lazy
Sheets, deceptive in the gently cross-hatched airs,
    And put into perspective by the wings of estuarial birds,
And the jetty, of course! long-planked & relaxed, soars
        beyond words.

An endless map for private concerns, gateway to weekend peace,
    The traffic streaming past forgotten with the first wooden squeak:
And residents are the first to call the police – who respond to this
    Neighbourhood Watch – if youths should sit & swing the feet, suck
On cigarettes & drink cheap plonk. South-west wine poured politely
And drunk from transparent glass, the buttocks cushioned
By a thickish mat, makes getting pissed legitimate, pity
        the kids 'stink'.

Canning Bridge

Linking the narrow neck with a classical bent,
    The confusion of pylon & crossbeam giving it mystery,
Bloodworms busy in the early morning, & mulloway running the persistent
    Tide – collecting the curvature of the 'pretty'
City – small enough to mock distance – the misty-eyed
    Morning, or gather all in like the lens of a camera,
While private school clubs urge their rowers to take pride
        in their task.

The Jetty Poems – 2
More Variations with Interpolations: 'Prologue' & 'Carmon figuratum'

Prologue

The line suffuses
the variegated purples
& reds becoming a deeply
sulphurous yellow
in the shallows.
I tell my son
that when I was young
I was obsessed with chemical
reactions, the clarity
& exposition
of interactions.

Gunbower Road Jetty

Where as a thirteen-year-old
I was stabbed & thrown into the

grey-brown water, my bike
anchoring me to the grey silt.

Now these grassed banks
that choke & narrow an always

thin beach force you onto
its freshly-laid planks

on their squat Buddha pylons.
Yes, here I come to meditate.

Paperbarks, childhood sentinels,
exquisitely grotesque & almost

begging to be flayed alive;
fat wooden boats limp

at their moorings, though the day
is too sharp for indolence.

Heron patiently point out vandals
in speedboats wrecking the surface,

dizzied by the flurry & crazy
mixing of ripples, light, and furrows

not showing it, though the bow waves
eventually drive them from their mounts.

Shibboleth that will not depress
the sad pollution of a relationship

cast like a lifebuoy from a jetty
perched over waters almost too shallow

to need it, and the tide high.
And time dragged thinly the heron's

trailing legs   lith   lith   lith
against the shadow of a breeze

or hissing slightly through burley cages
lodged between the planks; across

the river the furthest bank burns
with the frantic peak-hour traffic.

A rank of nasturtium flowers clinging
to the slopes expects to spark

as the day warms up & the micro-shape
of Gunbower Road jetty equivocates.

Rookwood Street Jetty

T-shaped with money to back it up,
all Esplanades seem wealthy,

though poorly kept & camouflaged
against the glare, this is the touch,

the simple life? Cormorants perched
on mountains of corrosive shit

mock clean cruisers moored a little
way out, lobbying with lazy sheets

the deceptive cross-hatched airs
that shape these waters and their

palisades of estuarial birds & paperbarks!
Long-planked, the endless map

suggests residents and polite couples
visiting via bikeways will one day

look much further than a closely
'distant' bank. This, for me, is absence,

and the river's gentle curve is wrecked
by this small jetty's subterfuge.

My incantations and expositions
will not bring you back.

Carmon figuratum

The shape is in the maybe or mightbe
of the words and not the layout or plan

as the page has little to do with this.
Scan lines and shape will emerge

like a boat sailing out of the gloom
of coloured dots, a kind of perceptual

testing ground that has you focussing
on some distant point to realise

it's there, right in front of your face.

envoi / Recollection

The line suffuses
the variegated purples
& reds becoming a deeply
sulphurous yellow
in the shallows.
I tell my son
that when I was young
I was obsessed with chemical
reactions, the clarity
& exposition
of interactions.

The Yellow Line Diathermy

Death holds a yellow line
double-ended bluntly, with
all the makings of a phlogistic
diagnosis blended with concrete.
Blood and concrete have much
in common, though no sign denotes
beyond a sign on either side
perched over the yellow line –
'No fishing beyond area marked
by yellow line.' Blood
links death below the surface,
reaches up and supports our feet
as we, in transit, refuse to recognise
their assistance. This stretch
of fisherman's paradise is walked
by the initiate and novice,
plumbing the sport with a wirework
of nylon line and flesh,
hangers of bone and lead, arched
high over the picaresque, the river
flowing and negotiating death,
reading the keel-hauled body
of trumpeter, gobble-gut,
and blowfish, the poison head
of catfish, the heat of veins
suspended, as if on this
      all life depended.

Chillies

1 *The Conservative*

Not supplicants but receptors –
wanton idols
raising red tribute, the crossover
green–orange, a query
in need of editing, ingesting the anger
and soil's biteback, the soil
drinking a market economy
red being more marketable
(a humorous colour), a conservative
hotbed wanting to cling
but conscious of the constituents'
response, hasten slowly.

2 *The Middle Ground*

Or chillies without seeds.
Rarely as hot, colour
as of chrysoprase, deeply attractive,
mimicking the wrought heart
of compassion.
You don't need a glass of water
even if you'd
like to think so.

3 *The Radical*

Green is the heat,
each chilli a piece,
sweat and a repeating stomach
something to flaunt.
You grow your own
but despite rumours
don't plant on the full moon.
Slim canisters
of motivation, slick grenades
imploding.

Residue

I am addicted
to chillies.
I break a red chilli
with my fingers
and spread it
through my meal.
Another false god
bringing its pleasures.

A friend needles me
another can barely
contain her laughter.
I wipe my eyes, a seed
lodges in a tear duct.
My tears are red
and pungent.
The seeds
are the hottest
part.

The Liberating Chillies

She hates them.
I'm addicted
grow my own
and am fascinated
by the way green turns
almost black before
the sun liberates
the red. My love
of the word 'wicked'
stems from chillies.
A bad experience
with bird's eyes

actually. Ah, little
bulls' horn rhytons,
quivers of fertility
permanently erect – the fruit
mocking the delicate flower.
But I burn
my self – the seeds
hold the sharpest power
and you must sacrifice
aesthetics for pleasure.
I burn from the inside out.

Chilli Hunt

She says that chillies
are a form of madness –
that like a crazed dog I froth
at the thought of them.
A bizarre addiction.

Maybe. Last night the moon,
full if slightly kinked,
marked a kris on the skins
of chillies bent towards
its grasp, fine metal reaching

for the loadstone. Ah that crazy
tattooist the moon. Chillies
are neither mad nor sane
if they show reverence for its
persistence. For today

I hunt without words. I feel
her watching over my shoulder,
skirts teasing the grass,
the skin on my back
erupting. I continue breaking

the stalks, collecting. Some
for immediate use, others for
drying. I know the full-blown

moon hunts in the back of her
eyes, that chillies a deeper red
than mine mark time and call her
to leave me to a minor harvest.

Chilli Catharsis

It fortifies my blood
against the heat
of separation –
a placebo.
Fire against fire.
Unleash your black
lightning: anti-sex,
space condensed ultra
or even collapsed.
I take I take.
This the poet
abusing language
for the sake of stasis –
the symbol as solid
as you wish. The devil's tool,
the devil's number.
Concrete. The sculpted
chilli. Like falling
on your own sword.
The heat the heat.
Fall into my burnt body
and torch your anger,
a chilli dance
for our son – fantasia
purified. Clean
but cold. Our sweat ice
on swollen cheeks. Chillies
charred at our feet.

Hereditary Chillies / Predestination

That in their infancy
the plants are so vulnerable
appeals to me – the leaf eaters
and sap suckers of the garden
will defoliate, destalk,
and wizen them before the sun
has risen. But fruiting,
they are rarely bothered.
But this of course is not
so remarkable when considered
comparatively. Vulnerability
heightens savagery – the cute
lion cub et al. The other
thing that fascinates me
is their sense of fait accompli –
but there is nothing in my
family tree to suggest
an onslaught of chilli.
Neither my mother nor father
can stomach them.

Archetypal Chillies

Are etched deep within
the human psyche – burning
seedcases bursting and re-locating
their ornamental hue. I open my
skull to your inquisitive gaze –
look, here are my chillies,
red and foreboding, hungry
for the light. See, you've done

me a favour – chillies breed on lies
but thrive on truth. They like it
both ways. Ah, if only
you'd admit to chillies – then,
then you'd understand me. The rhetoric
would flower superbly and I'd sing.
Christ, I'd sing. And you'd hear me
no matter where you hid. Your dreams
would be coloured by my song. Of chillies
and their involvement with the growth
of our souls. Of chillies and their
need for nurturing. Of the bitterness
they harvest from rejection. For this
is their strength – they are of you and I,
they are the sun's subtle rays
grown both cold and hot, they
like it both ways.

Transcendental Chillies

The weather's changing
so chillies redden
slowly. I do not expect
them to ripen according
to my program – though I'm
told this is my way.
But a few warm days
and you can be almost
guaranteed to find them
moving from state to state.
A green chilli flatlining
and finding the other side
tolerable. Easter Friday.
The heavy clouds are rolling in.
They predicted that a week ago.

Here, try a chilli – they're
deadly at this time of year –
the pride of the garden – corn
long since finished, the last rays
of summer spilling from overripe
tomatoes, lettuces shaking their
seedy arms, their heads embalmed
about thickened stalks
while chillies – majestic – daggers
awaiting the sunlight, hone
their skills in the weakening light.

The police busted me with a chilli in my pocket

It'd been through the wash – it was
in fact half-a-chilli
looking fibrous and not a little
washed out. But there was
no doubting it was a chilli,
I accepted that – no need
for laboratory tests, the eye
and honesty adequate analysis.
So, why do you do it
they asked. I dunno, just a habit
I guess. The sun dropped below
the horizon like a billiard ball.
The chilli glowed in a hand.
One of them rubbed his eyes and they
began to sting. We'll have you for assault
they said.

Red Data Book

1

The lists of endangered species
grow: if our love faces

extinction then growth
maligns itself & a word means

one thing while symbol-
ising another. Or maybe

we are in the early
evolutionary

stages – & this our body
is but a step

in the right
direction,

this poem
the missing link.

2

In the ambiguity
all passes

before we want
to realise

that an attempt
to save is ludicrous

while destroying
the habitat.

In Dryandra forest
numbats scratch out

a living. We assume
they are as conscious

of their bodies
as we are of ours

though can be
fairly certain

that they are unaware
of how vulnerable

they are
to outside influence.

Their lifespans
so short.

Instinct – an unreliable
if determined partner.

This is why poetry
is a substitute

for love & not
vice versa. This

is why the red data
is the proof copy

for an anthology
of vanquished species.

The Tiger Moth Poem

Prologue

High or low in the up & coming
Loop, the lift   lift   lift
Undercut & free of gravity:

Stress & tempestuous the cloud –
Material around the cowl & prop,
& the isolation as all eyes

Are fixed on you. And the sun
Low over your shoulder goading
You on & on & on, the blood

Too hot as a chill southern
Wind cuts past & you fly
By instinct, the instruments

All too crazy & the radio OUT.

1 *Distance*

Distant the lowland cutaway,
those mowed lines in the burn-back;
red clay compatible under

the painfully blue
autumn sky. It is seeding time
as I prepare to leave,

turn the climates upside down.
I leave the gneiss
& shale & lower

sheep jaws encased in fast-
setting mud, cat prints
hot-trotting the pyrographed

lines of finches burnt
into the moistening straw,
the burrows of seed gatherers

foxes calling like crazy toys
that have lost their heads, pilots
learning their 'tricks

of significance' in storming
the farmhouse roof, a windmill
centering the paddock.

I search for you. The compass's
tetchy needle disorientates
& the wind feints altitude.

I ground myself.

2   *Those fractured & tempestuous flakes of sunlight*

Darkness cannot seal the sky.
Highroller & naysayer
as night approaches

or bad weather sails
in from the coast. Joy
says stick it, hang in there.

I believe it. And can wait.

3   *An Aside*

Mount Bakewell prompts a flight
of cockatoos, furrows closely
cropped & sulphur crests

stirring flight as fear.
Ah, like snow ghosts
as blue as shadows

draped through leaves
they darken the road
with the intensity

of their navigations,
their individual brilliance
surrendered to instinct,

pandemonium, Babelic silos
coming unstuck, spilt grain
lighting the flock's heart.

4 *Sculpturing hearsay*

Once highrolling & sharp
& keeping it together
banks of wire
compile
a sculptural
ruse
as weekend pilots
pursue harmony
close to the ground
only to be dragged down
as the wire catches
their landing gear.

5 *Zoom*

Close-up you are as I
thought you might be;

focussed in your
secrecy.

6 *South*

Karri loam night-breathes.

Stars lift only to net
the canopy montage

while deeply emerald birds
rise vertically

dragging night backwards.

7 *A definition of space*

Positioning ourselves
between lovers,
delaying flights,
letting sleep shape
a life between the covers.

8 *Skippy Rock*

Ground to antimony
cuttlefish long-since
scuttled on Skippy Rock,
oystercatchers & sulky
fishhooks lodged between rock
& froth. A phalanx
of red rock crabs
backtracking as the swell
tests their grip & we
invoke freak waves
expecting them to tell
us something about our-
selves. A Tiger Moth
flies against the sun
& touches your
outstretched finger,

the whirr of its engine
an affirmation as love
inclines naturally
towards the möbius thread
binding rock & sea & air
& the brilliant red beaks
of the oystercatchers
pierce the pretty
picture.

9 (1) *Ascension*

Smoke sitting at thirty degrees
to an indigo sea
drives you inland
where swans familiar
with the chatter
of de Havilland
refuse to rise
from placid waters
that hold Molloy Island
firmly in their grip.
The best time is before the sun
drinks stars that have drunk the sea,
when cowboys are crashed out
& the larvae of tiger moths
sense wings stretching
over their bodies – the brilliance
of their markings suggesting
a delicate winter but one bitter
for predators. Time
cannot exceed 139 knots
per hour & the journey
must be worth its destination
as rivets & split pins spin wildly
in stall, climb, or cruise,
& the world of trawlers, nets, and jetties
is micro, & a brickred sunset is a wall
dissolving with an arrival
timed by flights
of pelicans.

9 (II)   *Even the sewage ponds look beautiful*

Even the sewage ponds
look beautiful from up here –
over the perfectly framed
& textured glassine
surface, discolouration
the mystery in a brilliantly vivid
Guy Grey-Smith
                    painting.

10   *'It was a store of the unspoken in the bird*
     that whirred the air, that every
                 occasion of the word
     overawed.'
          ROBERT DUNCAN

It is said over Sugarloaf Rock near the Cape
that a red-tailed tropic bird fails
                    to land & passes
its southern-

most breeding ground. That it flies against its instinct
to re-join its programmed flight, to
                    stir warming thermals
against the cold

words that define its plight. That you remain silent
as I recount the facts, the light
                    stripped back & season-less,
night-bound &

choked up.

11 *Anomalies*

Clouds deeply navy
disorientate & pin
tiger moths to spires.

Zinc clouds strung high lift
wing-torn tigermoths gently
from spires, just because.

Sun dials helipads
back flying to avoid spires
in life-saving flight.

12 *A Prayer of Thanks*

to sing with spirit & mind
that flesh is yours & penitent
& escaping the autolytic,
auto-da-fé,

the fuel that brought fire
without warmth,
the flight bound down
by topography,
that you taught me
to honour the body.

Motels

1 *City to Country*

They get excited not so much by the scene
but the smell of heavily perfumed soap
& crisp linen – the towels are cowhide
but this is seen as therapeutic to city skins.
A salesman who is sick to death
of room service & suitcases
thinks that maybe he's not so badly off –
a couple are fighting in the next room.
Though he laments the absence of call girls
in small coastal towns – the setting
so inviting, the sunsets passion-pink & perfect.
Tourist-info booklets sit on tables next to phones,
the breakfast hole-in-the-wall which has
always fascinated children who think they're
a long way further from home than they are,
who believe the food is spirited there.
The salesman is masturbating, the couple
are having noisy sex – 'I don't give a damn
if anyone hears, we've paid good money ...,'
breakfast finished, children pester parents
'what are we goin' to do now,' &
somebody switches on a television – LOUD.

2 *Country to City*

A double-gee piercing the ball of your foot
as you leave the bed with its hospital-tucked sheets
suggests that country lasses and lads
have been in the city, probably
raging out over the long weekend –
no b & s balls but nightclubs
& amphetamines, bombing
the motel pool at three
in the morning,
fucking on the flagstones,
dropping empties from the balcony.

The city is their playground
but as Sunday night approaches
they settle down, talk turning
to mornings on ploughs,
at roadhouses, in shearing sheds.

An Anecdote from the Orchardist

The pump was pushed into the brook
about six years ago – gibbering froth,
its bones picked for transplant,
the leftovers mangled with iron rods.
Polythene pipe still crisscrosses
the orchard though now perished
and split. His trees cower with each
passing summer. He asks me why people
have stopped going to church, what
has happened to God, as if God were
something he'd once recognised
in people's faces. And why they strip
fruit from the trees and crush
it underfoot, fill the brook until jam
stews in the rapids. Sometimes he cries
in front of them and says they've
only to ask and he'll give them bag on bag
of oranges, mandarins, and lemons,
of light and dark figs he planted thirty
years back along the narrow banks.
With a wet crack he'll crush a snail
with his walking-stick and meet my protests
with 'snails aren't animals', and then tell me
of the wagtails nesting in the saplings
by the front gate. He sees a new world coming –
the pea flowers already shining despite the grass
growing rank about them. The wagtails twitch.
The sun slides off the tin roof into the forty-four
full to the brim with water and rust.

                                        He collects
anecdotes, they help him forget the frustration
of being an orchardist in the city: at harvest
time the poorest of the village were seen
as the richest if they refused to work
the lands, the lands of the wealthy.
Once, I told him of the grapes of wrath,
of fruit and vegetables bulldozed into pits
while the army kept starving crowds at bay.
But this was my story, and he seemed
anxious to tell one of his own.

Lookout

Sliding down through the hills, exhaust
distorting the city, bindi-eyes of woodsmoke
catching the windscreen, the cut scarp
bleeding its heavy arterial clay
indifferently. Touring the catchment
you define a sense of place, memory
fracturing like poorly poured
dam walls or rammed earth
that's dissolving. When the body's chart
has been distorted by spies & assassins,
& you follow the altered terrain
so many times in your head, you read
the land like a ghost limb. Where maps
are past their 'use-by date', where
topography is a word from a lost language,
where surveying is neither a desire
nor a possibility. Somewhere around here
there's a lookout – the boundary between
catchment area & suburbia – a place to pause & take stock,
to read the legend: projection, scale, & white-tailed
black cockatoos auguring rain & change.

Swarm: The Sequel

As the fumes of three
different blooms swirl
enticingly
about the mouth
of the hive
a bristling ball
of bees rolls
soprano & spitting
static electricity
into the first
sunlight
in weeks, the bio–
thermostat moving
from steely cold
to full throttle
in minutes.
There is a delicate
calm in our house.
And for the first year
out of three
we do not read portents
into this swarming.
Even our child
retains his confidence.
It's okay he says,
they just hover
over the orange blossom
& disperse.

Wireless Hill

Not seen for decades, the parrot bush
makes a subtle comeback – fire
liberating seeds from their long

hibernation. A twenty-eight melds
into its birth flower, camouflaging
and buzzing and cackling out of sight:

a satellite lost in crazy telemetry,
untrackable despite an atmosphere
of communication. The sea-breeze, salty

and moist and full of static, zips
about the walkways and the triptych
of lookout towers, anchorage blocks

of Wireless Hill's original aerial.
With a festive glint on their bonnets,
cars unwind the radials, stereos

pursue their fractious circuits, trilling
and hissing like valve radios. And from
the central tower I look out over

Alfred Cove, and absorb the river.
You watch the children ski down slides
in the adventure playground and scoot

their bikes about the walkways, the sticky
hum that comes with rubber on hot concrete
reminding you of our son. You look

to the base of the tower, I look out –
even further than the river. But the sun
drives us towards the shade and touching

earth we hear the silent conversations
that crackle so faintly, too faint even
for aerials to detect. Yes, our son

would wade out into that cove,
over the rusty flats, bloodworms
unravelling and inciting black silt,

while pelicans, those navigation
markers for waders and migratory birds,
disappear in the space between sandbars.

On Entering Your Thirty-First Year
ref. Byron, Porter, Tranter et al.

The saturation of your art
despite trying to live outside your poetry
as ART yells harshly, 'It's just you
                trying hard to get out!' –

too exciting by half, the question is what to do (with)
this excess energy that seems to be
the signature – de rigueur – of the Age,
                or even recherché?

That you or they are satisfied with the echo
of the Master naming Names that might well
include your own, or in the very least, the name of some-
                one you could claim to 'know'

but unfortunately stuck with habits
no one wants to own, like keeping those mull
plants (stuck wanly on your sunless balcony,
                withering impolitely),

or going clothesless in the kitchen, 'wander-
lust' a catastrophe just waiting to happen:
the river coolly photogenic
                and too much like a line waiting to be

snorted. Unlike the discotheque's sullen
attraction, which is the animal in the
poem waiting to get out – though the phone
               brings the party to you.

But look, at thirty this is seen as keeping
it reasonably under control:
and as long as the lines keep writing themselves –
               which they don't – you won't need pay

for therapy or attend glum AA meetings.
Hey, scratch your meanings on a brown paper bag
that's been chock-a-block with nuts and cans
               and that will do for the scholar

or librarian: those nagging voices so strongly
coming on, that to avoid your avid Nature is danger –
calenture and betrayal of the facts,
               that nothing can trouble words

(roughly translated as the joy of life, just for you) –
the music not a scratch on Thrash or Goth
or even *The Magic Flute, Messiah,*
               or Iggy Pop's *Passenger.*

And money as imitation takes
liberties or dupes you into thinking that a nice bloke would
always give away his room to strangers
               and simultaneously con

a few grand out of his mother. Metrical
consistency is a poor excuse,
but things like this only show themselves with distance –
               the ear having nothing

to do with pissing yourself in public,
delirium tremens, or a solid
dose of pox to keep the machine on its toes;
               rather, a need to peruse

or be perused by almost perfect words
in almost perfect order – this comes
as a politically correct excuse
                    near as I can guess.

That only your lust for social
failure (raison d'être?) will drive
you beyond the abyss towards a spiritual bliss,
                    howling to the Feds,

as the Age will hopefully decree, some day:
these were inaugural signs of decay,
that worse was yet to come: music, painting,
                    and words as ART – per verse!

Dennis Hopper – Eulogy

Before his blue period & not near-
ly as slick, despite deep shit

burning crazy & aggressive in THOSE
eyes, & that vicious 'we're sinking but we'll

all go down with the fucking ship' slant
on his hat that is more than angel dust

whizzing through his velveteen blood.
Yeah, Frank, the audience is with you,

breathe deep & fuck, fuck Frank,
it's a clown of a life.

Virtual Reality

Like a snow job in a desert –
she takes it with a pinch of salt:
on face value you might call
a halt to this life that up till now
has rolled on like an underarm
deodorant with a full
quota of aluminium.
Like reading Pope & Dryden
without realising their link
to Tom Cruise & Nicole Kidman,
Madonna & Don King.
Yep, it's a con she says
to the television. Her husband
grunts in the background
& swivels a baked potato
on its cushion of gravy.
Gotta wake up to myself
& skip the iceblocks –
just because the mercury's up
it doesn't mean I've got
to embellish the mystery.
It's enough that I'm here –
crazy for a cup of tea
& a dose of virtual reality.

Grotesque: an elegy & a parody

(for John Forbes)

State of the art bad taste, a modern hybrid gothic.
Grotesque is going to a party with Kyle & the boys.
It's smoking dope amongst a pod of go–getters
        pumping their fatuous ecstasy grins.

Or the girl that tells you a good friend is two bolts
Short of Frankenstein after you've realised that watching
Alien 3 is like touring your bowel while it's haemorrhaging.
        That the guy next to you on the bus

Has a bullet-shaped head with a newspaper spread like
How-to-use instructions. But then there's High Grotesque,
Which doesn't rely on the politics of abuse or one-up-man-
        ship: the anti-bourgeois elites

Feeling comfortable on their un-sprung couches. No, High
Grotesque is recognising the art of diminished living
As an art obtainable only via the School of Alcohol Ism.
        It's reading the vomit you'd deposited

On the step the night before as 'take the train to Fremantle
& touch that friendly barmaid you met a couple of weeks ago
For a loan, or failing that, to hock your mother's
        portable stereo' – a present from you.

smith-corona elect

connects the plasticity of language and metal,
the four pulses of a navigation light with the five
pulses of its optical silence, an electric whirr
must persist. this, john tranter's first typewriter,
feeds the paper actualities – a mouse moves rapidly
over the floor of an eighth storey apartment and i
entreat skills laid in a mixture of naive delusion
and past intoxications, i entreat a myomancy
which comes out of divining and dedicate this
first-off-the-rank sheet of bank to john's poem
about gin and all that seen within puddles intentional
and unintentional, and i dedicate it to the joy
of a weather person on television (this is out
of character for me as I rarely watch tv) who seemed
pleased that today's ultraviolet levels were low
despite it being the warmest june day since 1956.
the sails of the opera house retract as you
move further away, the waves absorbing and the captain
of the ferry altering the pace in an effort to iron
out the vibrations ringing the hull. at milson's point
grace cossington-smith's curve of the bridge whittles
or gouges chips/flecks out of mortar, sky, metal, a wooden
transom, an illusion that should have occurred
earlier in the poem, before the keys hammered home
their message without the aid of fingers, before
rhythm and melody succumbed to the twin terrors
of spontaneity and enthusiasm. the ribbon contains
its coded message smith-corona elect, masterpiece
of engineering, glory of the year 1956, a great year
that gave us...

Warhol at Wheatlands

He's polite looking over the polaroids
saying gee & fantastic, though always
standing close to the warm glow

of the Wonderheat as the flames
lick the self-cleansing glass.
It's winter down here & the sudden

change has left him wanting. Fog
creeps up from the gullies & toupées
the thinly pastured soil. It doesn't

remind him of America at all. But there's
a show on television about New York so
we stare silently, maybe he's asleep

behind his dark glasses? Wish Tom
& Nicole were here. He likes the laser
prints of Venice cluttering the hallway,

the sun a luminous patch trying
to break through the dank cotton air
& the security film on the windows.

Deadlocks & hardened glass make him feel
comfortable, though being locked inside
with Winchester rifles has him tinfoiling

his bedroom – he asks one of us but we're
getting ready for seeding & can't spare a moment.
Ringnecked parrots sit in the fruit trees

& he asks if they're famous. But he
doesn't talk much (really). Asked about Marilyn
he shuffles uncomfortably – outside, in the

spaces between parrots & fruit trees
the stubble rots & the day fails
        to sparkle.

Shot Marilyns & Gunbelt

Like night sight in a world
of glittering parasites

Marilyn dies another
half-a-dozen times

at least. I consider
the multiplicity

of a thick atmosphere,
space, the collectables

in this house
& surrounding grounds

beyond which crops
have broken unglazed surfaces

& good follow-up rains
are expected. Powerlines

hiss in the uneasy air –
like poems escaping from screen-prints –

& a gunbelt hangs
in the kitchen.

And the weapon's calibre
that killed Marilyn

over & over,
pro rata?

Well, these are merely 22s
though prints of Pop muzzle

family snapshots
in the hallway.

The sunset is tacky
& nothing is special.

On Warhol's *Camouflage Statue of Liberty*
& Being Refused Entry into the United States
by US Immigration

'les hons biscuits', ah, FABIS, the greatest
of gifts, the blood of/and as freedom,

Libertarian – if you look closely
she might tap dance, God forbid the can-can –

they suffered the strong fragrance but didn't
inhale the brand name: Liberty (luck):

'Have Gun/Will Shoot'; Repent AND SIN NO
MORE! And these untitled? No decay

& the ancien régime is 'trendy'
(which is a frozen & suitably bor-

ing word when not in constant use). Solar-
isation a pissy example – in some States

you'd hold no record & Immigration
wouldn't give a shit. Paul Hogan is THERE!

Night Seeding & Notions of Property

Dizzy with figure-eighting
the corners of his fields, the drills
filled with seed & super

and closed over under
the tattooed rash of night,
foxes' muffling barks

& fighting to cover tracks
with a starpicket the axis
of a compass whose North

is wire-guided & lethal: silver
tennis balls exploding in their spiralled
swing on totem-tennis poles

for here stillness shivers & moves
like frost moves the shattered
flesh of quartz

over the wasted plots. A clear
dawn is soluble anyway
& the tractor gnaws,

its queasy stomach
turning slowly & coldly
with winter:

        dispossessed
the farmer moans – a sudden downpour
shaves his precious topsoil.

The ghosts clamour about the microwave
& television set, the stove broods
in this sauna of politeness.

City people are expecting billy tea
& damper & the sheep to bleat
in unison. Nous regrettons parler.

There wasn't a kangaroo to be seen.
Night-seeding, the tractor's floodlights
are blood-red & ovarian –

nurturing the cloddish soil, & always
the farmer working the wheel, hands
gnarled & frostbitten & large.

Skeleton weed / generative grammar

I *Finite-state*

The "i" takes in what is said—
yes, it is easily led
across the floors of discourse
only to find itself a force
easily reckoned with: there's
no point in stock-taking arrears
as fleshly interests tell you
nothing except acceptability & taboo.
Take skeleton weed infesting
the crop – rosette of basal
leaves unleashing a fatal
stem with *daisy-like* flowers
that drop (into) parachute clusters
of seeds. One missed when
they scour the field (men
& women anonymously-clothed
seated on a spidery raft dragged
behind a plodding tractor,
monotony testing the free-will factor),
can lead to disaster.

II *Phrase-structure*

{[((analys)ing)] [the ((constituent)s)]}
we examine(?) the wool of sheep
for free-loading skeleton-weed seeds,
their teeth specifically designed
for wool: the ag department
have decided they ARE selective
though admit our investigations
will help their "research".

III *transformational*

One year the farmer asked us if we
felt guilty for missing one & hence ruining
his would-have-been bumper crop.
Quarantined the following year. Losing
his unseeded would-be bumper crop.
Ruining his credit rating. His marriage.
His son's & daughter's places
at their exclusive city boarding
schools. His problem with alcohol.
His subsequent breakdown
& hospitalisation. (?) We remained
& still remain passive. We still remain
& remained passive. Still we remained
& remain passive. But we [look(ed)] deeply,
collectively & independently
into our SELVES. Our silence
was an utterance of a loud inner speech.
A loud inner speech was an utterance
of our silence. Speaking for myself,
I've included in my lexicon of guilt
the following: what I feel today
will I feel tomorrow? And those tight
yellow flowers: so beautiful on the wiry
structures they call "skeleton weed".

John Kinsella was born in Perth, Western Australia, in 1963. He studied at The University of Western Australia and travelled extensively for a number of years through Europe, the Middle East, and Asia. After returning to Western Australia he lived in various suburban and rural areas and had various jobs. He is the founding editor of the international poetry magazine *Salt*. He now lives in Cambridge and divides his time between Britain and Australia; he is a By-Fellow of Churchill College.

John Kinsella has published poems in a large number of literary journals in Australia, the USA, Britain, New Zealand, Japan, India and Canada. He has published twelve collections of poetry in Australia, and four books in Britain: *The Silo* and *The Undertow: New & Selected Poems* from Arc, and *Poems 1980-1994* and *The Hunt and other poems* from Bloodaxe. His many prizes include the John Bray Award for Poetry from the Adelaide Festival.

He has given readings of his work in Britain, Ireland, the USA, Spain, France and Germany. He has received writing grants from both the Western Australian Department for the Arts and the Literature Board of the Australia Council. In 1996 he received a Young Australian Creative Fellowship and has recently been awarded a two-year Fellowship from the Literature Board of the Australia Council.